NAMIBIA
The Facts

International Defence & Aid Fund
104 Newgate Street, London EC1
September 1980

Published 1980

The International Defence and Aid Fund for Southern Africa is a humanitarian organisation which has worked consistently for peaceful and constructive solutions to the problems created by racial oppression in Southern Africa.

It sprang from Christian and humanist opposition to the evils and injustices of apartheid in South Africa. It is dedicated to the achievement of free, democratic, non-racial societies throughout Southern Africa.

The objects of the Fund are:–

(i)   to aid, defend and rehabilitate the victims of unjust legislation and oppressive and arbitrary procedures,

(ii) to support their families and dependents,

(iii) to keep the conscience of the world alive to the issues at stake.

In accordance with these three objects, the Fund distributes its humanitarian aid to the victims of racial injustice without any discrimination on grounds of race, colour, religious or political affiliation. The only criterion is that of genuine need.

For many years, under clause (iii) of its objects, the Fund has run a comprehensive information service on affairs in Southern Africa. This includes visual documentation. It produces a regular news bulletin 'FOCUS' on Political Repression in Southern Africa, and publishes pamphlets and books on all aspects of life in Southern Africa.

The Fund prides itself on the strict accuracy of all its information.

This book was prepared by IDAF Research, Information and Publicity Department

ISBN No. 0 904759 41 5

Contents

I Facts and figures

The name Namibia derives from the word Namib, meaning "the enclosure" in the Nama language. The Namib desert, which stretches along the west coast of the territory, forms a natural shield which for a long time protected the interior from intruders.

The German colonists called the territory German South West Africa, and the South African occupying regime retained that name, dropping the prefix.

The different names reflect conflicting political positions in the international dispute over the territory. Those favouring the country's independence as a sovereign and united state call it Namibia. A United Nations General Assembly resolution affirmed in June 1968 that, in accordance with the desires of the people, South West Africa should be known as Namibia, thus enshrining the name in international law. The great majority of black people associate the name South West Africa with colonial oppression and refer to their country as Namibia.

Recently, the name "South West Africa/Namibia" has been used in the press and on identity documents issued by the South African-appointed Administrator General on the grounds that a decision to that effect was taken in 1977. This has brought strong protests from some extreme right-wing groups.[1]

GEOGRAPHY

Namibia is a vast territory in the south-western part of the continent of Africa, stretching along the South Atlantic coast. The total area of Namibia covers 824,295 km sq (317,827 square miles), nearly four times the size of the United Kingdom. It shares a 1,600 km long border in the north with Angola. In the east it borders on Botswana, and in the south and south east on the Cape Province of the Republic of South Africa. The Caprivi Strip, a 64 km wide corridor stretching deep into the border area between Zambia and Botswana, is part of Namibia.

The main physical features of the territory are the extensive desert areas and the low overall rainfall. The Namib desert along the Atlantic coast covers approximately one-fifth of the total surface and is between 80 and 100 km wide; the Kalahari desert stretches along the border with Botswana. The Central Plateau, ranging in altitude between 1,000 and 2,000 metres, comprises more than 50% of the total area. It attracts little rain, and then only during three months of the year.

The territory lacks perennial rivers. The only permanent rivers are the Orange on the southern border with South Africa, and two northern rivers, the Cunene and Okavango, which are shared with Angola.

NATURAL RESOURCES

Namibia's basic natural resources are land, fish and minerals. While low rainfall and delicate soil structure hamper soil cultivation at present, the potential for agriculture is rated high. The Central Plateau is suitable for sheep and cattle grazing.

The country has the richest inshore and deepwater fishing zones in tropical Africa. The main inshore fish are pilchard and anchovy, the main deepwater fish is hake. Overfishing has led to a depletion of stock, but careful husbandry would restore this rich resource.

A wide range of minerals is found in Namibia. Diamonds are still its most important asset, but large-scale uranium mining is taking place which will ensure Namibia's place as the world's fifth largest uranium producer.[2] Other base metals include large deposits of copper, zinc and lead, while minor mineral products include cadmium, lithium, tin, silver, wolfram and salt.

Offshore oil prospecting is being carried out with the hope of significant finds. Natural gas has been discovered off the coast which may be used as a motor fuel. Namibia's mineral wealth makes it of strategic importance in international relations.

POPULATION

The size of the Namibian population is variously estimated, depending on whose figures are used.

A study for the United Nations Institute for Namibia concluded in 1978 that the population is probably 1,250,000, made up of slightly over 100,000 Europeans, 115,000 Coloureds, and 1,035,000 Africans.[3] Another researcher estimates a total population of between 950-1,010,000, with 850-900,000 blacks, and 100-110,000 whites.[4] Official South African statistics give the population as much smaller (753,000 blacks and 99,000 whites according to 1974 official estimates).[5] South African population figures are unreliable, as smaller estimates can be used to disguise how little South Africa is spending per head on social services, education etc.

South African statistics put a heavy emphasis on the different black "ethnic groups", reflecting the South African policy of fragmenting the black population into separate "nations". (see Ch. IV for detailed figures). South Africa presents the white population as a homogeneous group, although linguistically and culturally it divides into several groups, comprising an estimated 20,000 German speaking, 15,000 English and Portuguese speaking and 55,000 Afrikaans speaking people.[6]

6

II History

The original Namibians were the San (Bushmen) who lived as hunters and gatherers in small kinship groups throughout the subcontinent. From the early 17th century, the Herero and Nama, traditionally cattle farmers who held land, water and fishing grounds in common, are thought to have entered the area. The Damara, who probably arrived with the Nama, worked as herdsmen among them and the Hereros. In the north, relatively isolated, lived the pastoral Ovambos who grew maize and kept cattle. They were the largest, and the only predominantly agricultural tribe, producing a surplus which enabled craftsmen such as blacksmiths, potters and woodcarvers to develop their skills.

During the early 19th century, a group of christianised Namas, the Orlam, returned from further south under pressure from white colonial expansion in the Cape. Their centralised political structure and superior weapons enabled them to subjugate the Hereros temporarily and take over their grazing lands. Afrikaans-speaking descendants of whites and Namas in the Cape, called Basters, moved into the area of Nama settlement near Windhoek.

At the time of European arrival, the inhabitants of the area had developed social and political systems at different stages. Collective ownership of natural resources prevailed. While grazing rights were a frequent cause for dispute, the concept of individual ownership and the large-scale dispossession of land were only introduced by the intruding whites.[1]

Namibia's rich pre-colonial history is used by South Africa today to justify its apartheid policy. This ignores the development of a multi-cultural society into one nation through the experiences of colonial oppression and the struggle for national liberation.

FIRST CONTACTS WITH WHITES

Early European exploration of the territory now known as Namibia began a new era which led to a quarrel among the imperialist powers over colonial control while the needs and interests of the indigenous people were ignored.

The Portuguese navigator Diago Cão was first to land on the Namibian coast in 1484, followed by other Portuguese, Dutch and British expeditions. These became more frequent after the British took over the administration of the Cape Colony from the Dutch in 1795. Missionary stations were established in the territory, closely followed by an increase in the number of traders who also brought alcohol and weapons, and introduced a money economy. This led to growing indebtedness among local people, and cattle thefts increased.

In 1878, the British annexed Walvis Bay. By 1884, it had come under the administration of the Cape. By this time, the Germans, who were late comers in the scramble for colonial conquest, were competing for territorial acquisitions, fearing that otherwise the remaining territories would be shared out by their rivals. In 1883, the German businessman F. A. E. Lüderitz purchased through an agent the Bay of Angra Pequena and a strip of land around it from a Nama chief, in return for 2,000 marks and a few old muskets. In the ensuing quarrel over German and British claims the Germans extended their control inland through "treaties of protection" with rival chiefs.

An Anglo-German Agreement in July 1890 shared the spoils. German South West Africa was created, but Britain retained Walvis Bay. The Caprivi Strip was included in the German territory, giving free access to the Zambezi which the Germans believed, erroneously, to be navigable to the east coast.

COLONIAL OCCUPATION

The Germans never established complete control over the entire colony, leaving the northern regions unpoliced. They imposed an iron rule over the Herero and Nama areas however. These are still known as the Police Zone.

German colonial troops increased from 250 in 1892 to 1,500 in 1904 and 15,000 in 1905 in the course of the wars fought against the indigenous people.[2]

German colonialism was characterised by the progressive alienation of land and cattle from the indigenous inhabitants, the ruthless repression of resistance, and the creation of a dispossessed African wage-labour force.

White settlement was on a small scale until after 1900. In 1897 there were about 1,050 German settlers and traders in Namibia. By 1913, the total white population, most of whom were Germans, comprised 14,840. Of the male white productive population in 1911, 17% were settlers, 29% workers and craftsmen, 33% government and army officials and 21% traders and missionaries.[3]

Vast tracts of land were alienated under the guise of treaties of protection signed by local chiefs; traders offered the Hereros worthless goods for their cattle. For instance, they would give five pounds of poor quality gunpowder for a big ox.[4] At the end of 1903, the Africans' land had been reduced to 31.4 million hectares out of a total land area of 83.5 million hectares. The rest was divided between concession companies, the colonial government and white settlers.[5] The Hereros' cattle stock was further reduced by foot and mouth disease from approximately 100,000 in the early 1890's to 46,000 in 1902. German-owned cattle were saved by inoculation and numbered 44,500. There were 80,000 Hereros compared to 1,051 German settlers and traders.[6]

A German leader of the Settlement Commission in the territory spelt out clearly German policy:

"the native tribes must withdraw from the lands on which they have pastured their cattle and so let the white man pasture his cattle on these self-same lands."[7]

AFRICAN PRIMARY RESISTANCE

Colonial exploitation led to the growth of resistance movements which were the forerunners of the modern national liberation movement in Namibia. Early uprisings were fragmented and were crushed, but they laid the basis for future unity.

In 1892, Germans attacked the settlement of the Nama leader, Kaptein Hendrik Witbooi, massacring about 150 people. A guerilla war lasting 1½ years followed. Throughout the 1890's different groups rebelled unsuccessfully.

In January 1904, the Herero rose up against German rule. 7-8,000 Herero fought for several months in open battles, but were hampered by their lack of arms and by their large cattle herds. By the end of August 1904, the entire Herero people were driven into the Omaheke desert and thousands massacred by German troops. The German Commander, von Trotha, had issued an extermination order:

"The Herero people must depart from the country. If they do not, I shall force them to, with large cannons. Within the German boundary every Herero, whether found armed or unarmed, with or without cattle, will be shot."[8]

16,000 Hereros survived out of a total population of about 60,000.[9] The Nama joined the uprising too late in August 1904, but continued a guerilla war until they were forced to sign a peace treaty in 1907. The survivors were obliged to do hard labour in prison camps, where many died.[10]

GERMAN RULE

German military victory was a prelude to the political control and economic exploitation of the indigenous population of Namibia.

The Herero and Nama were dispossessed of all their land and their social and political structures were shattered. A series of native decrees was enacted between 1906 and 1907 forbidding Africans to acquire land or cattle, forcing them to carry passes and face punishment for vagrancy if they could not prove employment. These measures were successful in forcing Africans into wage labour for white employers. By 1912, only 200 Herero and Nama were without paid employment. Under an ordinance introduced in 1886, "natives" could be flogged by colonial officials or farmers with no recourse to justice. The law differentiated at all levels between Africans and whites. Mixed marriages were forbidden.

THE LEAGUE OF NATIONS MANDATE

As a result of the First World War, Germany ceased to be a colonial power. In 1915, South African troops acting under British orders occupied the German colony of South West Africa, bringing it under South African military rule until the Treaty of Versailles in 1919.

South Africa intended to annex the territory. While the British war cabinet agreed, opposition from the United States President resulted in a compromise. South Africa would instead administer the territory under a "C" mandate of the League of Nations on behalf of Britain. Its duty, laid down in the Mandate, was to prepare the territory for eventual self-determination and to "promote to the utmost the material and moral wellbeing and the social progress of the inhabitants."[11] South Africa's only concrete duty was to submit annual reports to the League of Nations. In reality, South Africa considered the Mandate merely as a gesture towards international understanding and proceeded to incorporate Namibia effectively into the Union of South Africa

Even before the Mandate had been signed, control was extended to Ovamboland, and the Ovambo chief Mandume was killed in 1917 by South African troops. Ovamboland was conquered and divided between Portugal and South Africa.

SOUTH AFRICAN RULE UNDER
THE LEAGUE OF NATIONS MANDATE

South African occupation of Namibia resulted in further entrenchment of the policies of land alienation, violent repression of protest and social and political restrictions imposed on the indigenous population.

Requests by the Herero people for the return of their land were rejected. Instead, they were given 800,000 hectares of the same Omaheke (sandveld) where thousands had perished in 1904. White South Africans were offered generous incentives to settle in Namibia. Nearly all viable farming land was reserved for and taken by whites. By 1928, the white population in Namibia reached 28,000, double the 1913 figure.[12]

Like the Germans before them, the South African regime introduced laws to restrict Africans' political rights and ensure a cheap supply of labour. Vagrancy laws prescribed punishment for Africans leaving their areas except to work for a white person. The *Master and Servants Proclamation* of 1920 prescribed punishments for neglect of duty, desertion from a job etc., and the *Native Administration Proclamation* of 1922 introduced the Pass Laws, requiring all blacks travelling outside their area to have a permit and show it on demand to any policeman.

Frequent uprisings against South African repression were brutally crushed. In 1922 the Bondelswarts, a small mixed Nama community, rose in revolt. Most of their land had been confiscated by the Germans and they survived by hunting wild animals with packs of dogs. A high dog tax was imposed by the South African government to force them to seek work as farm labourers. This and other measures threatening their livelihood finally led them to protest by retreating into a laager on a hill top. They were attacked by South African troops with machine guns and bombed by military aircraft. Over a hundred Bondelswarts were killed.

III   The International Status of Namibia

SOUTH AFRICA AND THE UNITED NATIONS

Namibia has become the subject of an international dispute concerning South Africa's occupation of the country. South Africa's interpretation of its role, and its *de facto* annexation of Namibia, have been pronounced illegal in international law.

Countries administering League of Nations Mandates agreed to enter into trusteeship agreements with the United Nations after the latter's establishment in 1945. These were intended to lead to the granting of full independence to the mandated territories. South Africa's demand for full incorporation of Namibia into the Union was rejected by the United Nations General Assembly. South Africa subsequently refused to enter into a Trusteeship agreement and in 1949 ceased submitting the reports required by the terms of its Mandate

In an effort to clarify the status of the territory, the United Nations requested advisory opinions from the International Court of Justice on several occasions. In 1960, Ethiopia and Liberia, then the only two African members of the United Nations, instituted legal proceedings against South Africa claiming that it had violated the Mandate by introducing apartheid in Namibia. These initiatives failed to resolve the dispute over the territory, however.

In its first ruling in 1950, the International Court of Justice held that the Mandate was still in force and that South Africa could not unilaterally alter the status of Namibia, but that it had no obligation to enter into a trusteeship agreement. On Liberia and Ethiopia's claims it ruled in 1966 that the petitioners had not established any legal right in the matter, and refused to rule on the substance of the matter.

The Court's 1966 ruling proved a watershed in Namibian politics. Namibians who had petitioned the United Nations for their independence since 1946 were shocked; and the South West Africa People's Organisation (SWAPO), formed in 1960, saw no alternative but to turn to armed struggle.[1] The Afro-Asian group at the United Nations became more insistent in its demand for international action.

As a result of these pressures, the United Nations General Assembly adopted Resolution 2145 (XXI) in October 1966 which terminated South Africa's Mandate and placed Namibia under direct United Nations control.

In March 1969, the United Nations Security Council endorsed this, declaring South African occupation of Namibia illegal and calling on South Africa to withdraw immediately its administration from the territory. The resolution called for international diplomatic and economic isolation of South Africa whenever it acted on behalf of Namibia. (Resolution 264).

In June 1971, the International Court of Justice finally confirmed this resolution, in an advisory opinion.

NAMIBIA'S STRATEGIC SIGNIFICANCE

South Africa's determination to retain control over Namibia reflects the strategic importance of the territory.

As a source of wealth, Namibia possesses minerals which are vital for the industrial development of South Africa. South Africa obtains uranium, diamonds, gold, copper and other minerals from Namibia both for its own consumption and for re-export.

Much of the nuclear development taking place in Europe assumes an uninterrupted supply of uranium. South Africa maintains strict control over uranium production, and Namibia contributes a third of all South Africa's uranium exports.

At a military level, South Africa uses the West's concern to protect the Cape sea route as a bargaining point in discussion about Namibia's future. To protect its own apartheid structures, South Africa sees Namibia as a buffer zone against the influence of neighbouring black African states and uses the territory as a base for military attacks into Angola and Zambia. With the victory of the national liberation movements in Zimbabwe, South Africa's determination to retain control over Namibia has hardened. (see Ch. XII).

WALVIS BAY

South Africa's annexation of Walvis Bay, geographically part of Namibia, is part of its strategy to maintain control in the country and defy international law. The United Nations Security Council declared in July 1978 that Namibian territorial integrity and unity must be ensured through the reintegration of Walvis Bay into the territory. (Res. 432).

Walvis Bay has a chequered history. An area of 434 square miles around the enclave was annexed by Britain in 1878, administered by the old Cape Colony from 1884 and later by the Union of South Africa. In 1922, the administration of Walvis Bay was handed to the mandated territory of South West Africa.[2] During negotiations for Namibian independence with the United Nations in 1977, South Africa unilaterally transferred the administration of Walvis Bay to the Cape Province,[3] placing it under Pretoria's direct jurisdiction.

Walvis Bay is of great strategic and economic importance. It is Namibia's only deep-water port, handling 90% of its overall export trade.[4] It is the centre of Namibia's fishing industry, and has been the base for extensive exploration for oil and natural gas.

South Africa's retention of Walvis Bay would provide a stranglehold over an independent Namibia. There is a fast-expanding South African airforce base in the enclave at Rooikop. A newly formed counter-insurgency section of the South African navy, the Marines, have been installed in Walvis Bay as part of a South African plan for the land and seaward defence of all ports.[5] One of the South African Defence Force's elite units, 2 South African Infantry Battalion Group, which is the only combined infantry/armour unit, is also based in the area.

THE UNITED NATIONS COUNCIL FOR NAMIBIA

Following the United Nations decision in 1966 to terminate South Africa's Mandate, the General Assembly established the United Nations Council for Namibia as the legal Administering Authority of Namibia and the policy-making organ at the United Nations. The Council's task is to administer the country until independence. At present, the Council has 31 members.[6] Among its many functions are to help Namibian refugees, organise a training programme for Namibians, issue travel documents and establish an emergency programme to render economic and technical assistance to Namibia.[7] A United Nations Fund for Namibia was established in 1970 to finance these activities.

The United Nations Institute for Namibia was opened in Lusaka in 1976 to prepare the ground for the rebuilding of an independent Namibia. The Institute provides Namibians with facilities for civil service and administration training and for research into the economic and social problems of reconstruction which will face a future independent country, such as transforming the economy, the labour system, education and other social services. 400 Namibians were training at the Institute in 1980.[8]

Other activities of the Council include co-operation with other United Nations agencies, for example under the "Nationhood Programme" for Namibia which was approved by the United Nations General Assembly in December 1976 (Res. 31/153). In May 1978, a planning workshop considered project proposals submitted by the UN specialised agencies, and in June 1978, 77 pre-independence project proposals were approved by the Council for Namibia.[9] By May 1979, 25 projects, including fellowships to train specialists in various aspects of mining, transport, statistics etc., were adopted by several United Nations agencies.[10]

IV South African Powers and Policies

SOUTH AFRICAN RULE OF LAW

South Africa has extended its own repressive laws and apartheid policies to Namibia both directly and through control over local institutions. While appearing to delegate powers to bodies in the territory, it has in fact retained a tight hold over all important matters. Under the *Treaty of Peace* and the *South West Africa Mandate Act*, 1919, the functions of administration were delegated by the South African Parliament to the Governor General. He exercised his functions through the Administrator of South West Africa, appointed by the South African government. In January 1921, the Administrator appointed an all-white Advisory Council.

The *South West Africa Constitution Act* of 1925 (No. 42) established an all-white Legislative Assembly for the territory, consisting of six members appointed by the Administrator and approved by the Governor General, and twelve elected members. Africans were not qualified to vote. The powers of the Legislative Assembly were negatively defined, specifying "scheduled" matters reserved to the South African Parliament on which the Legislative Assembly could not act. These included, notably, African affairs, railways and harbours, matters affecting civil servants, matters affecting the courts of justice and their procedure, postal, telegraph and telephone services, military organisation, immigration, custom and excise, and currency and banking matters.[1] The Legislative Assembly's powers were largely illusory. They were subordinate to those of the South African Parliament, whose Acts would prevail in the case of conflict. Ordinances of the Assembly on matters on which it could legislate, such as white education, roads, social welfare and health, required the assent of the Administrator who acted on instructions from the Governor General of South Africa.

The South African Parliament could legislate for the territory in regard to reserved matters, and the South African Governor General could issue Proclamations on any subject not within the jurisdiction of the Legislative Assembly. This complex structure disguised the fact that full and final administrative and legislative authority was vested with the government of South Africa. Despite numerous amendments and changes, this situation still pertains today.

With the victory of the National Party in South Africa in 1948, South Africa's occupation of Namibia was further entrenched. White Namibians, all members of the South West Africa National Party, were now represented in the South African Parliament, thus strengthening the new government in the Union of South Africa. The bantustan policy introduced by the National Party government in South Africa was applied to Namibia, and a battery of repressive laws, includ-

14

ing the *Suppression of Communism Act*, the *Terrorism Act* and the *Public Safety Act* were extended to the territory. Through most of the period and at the present time, the South African President could make laws in Namibia by Proclamation.

Legislation was passed in 1968 and 1969 to implement the bantustan programme. The *South West African Affairs Act* of 1969 (No. 25) removed 25 broad classes of subjects from the jurisdiction of the white Legislative Assembly, returning them to the jurisdiction of the South African Parliament and the State President.

This was in preparation for establishing "homeland authorities" for different "ethnic groups" as outlined in the bantustan programme. The *Development of Self-Government for Native Nations in South West Africa Act* of 1968 (No. 54) implemented the programme in so far as it dealt with "native affairs" in the territory.

SOUTH AFRICA'S BANTUSTAN POLICY

South Africa formally imposed its apartheid policy of dividing the country into separate "homelands" on Namibia in 1964, following a report and recommendations by a Commission of Inquiry into South West Africa appointed in 1962.

The Odendaal Plan, as the report became known, suggested dividing Namibians into twelve "population groups" — whites, Coloureds, Rehoboth Basters, Namas, Damaras, Hereros, Kaokovelders, Ovambos, Kavangos, Caprivians, Tswanas and Bushmen. Each black group, with the exception of the Coloureds, should occupy a "homeland". The "homelands" are Namibian analogues of the South African bantustans.

The Development of Self-Government for Native Nations in South West Africa Act (1968) provided for the creation, for each bantustan, of a legislative council with nominal ordinance-making powers and an executive council with corresponding administrative powers. The State President could establish a legislative council for any "native nation", which might enact laws on some 50 subjects within the "homeland" including education, welfare, clinics, establishment of business undertakings, roads, administration of justice, agriculture, labour bureaux, taxes and control of revenue funds. No legislative council is empowered to legislate on scheduled matters such as military, police, foreign affairs and amendment or repeal of the Act itself. The State President must approve any enactment before it becomes law, and he retains the right in all cases to amend or repeal new legislation.

The Act also empowered the State President to create tribal, community or regional "authorities" for African areas not under a legislative council. Extensive amendments to the Act were made by the *Development of Self-Government for Native Nations Amendment Act* of 1973 (No. 20) which enabled "homelands" to become "self-governing" as a transitional phase prior to "independence". The State President can declare a "homeland" a self-governing area, though the powers of the legislative council are not widened significantly. A "self-governing" area has a "cabinet" consisting of a "chief minister" and other "ministers" drawn from the legislative council.

Even if a "homeland" has become "self-governing", the State President may legislate by Proclamation and may overrule any contrary enactment by a legislative council. There have been recent moves to further strengthen this structure despite international condemnation of South Africa's bantustan policy (See Ch. XIII, *Alternative Strategies*).

APARTHEID PHILOSOPHY

The fragmentation of the country into separate "nations" is based on the claim that there exist different ethnic groups, each with specific tribal institutions, and that separate development ensures the harmonious progress of these groups towards "self determination".

In effect, the aims of the bantustan policy, which parallels that imposed on Africans in South Africa, are:

* to divide the Namibian nation along racialist lines and foster tribal divisions through South African-promoted "ethnic" governments.
* to suppress the consciousness of national unity which has grown historically from the early anti-colonial revolts.
* to ensure a continuous supply of cheap African labour to the white economy by forcing people into arid, small "homelands" which cannot sustain the population.
* to deprive black people of any rights in the "white areas" where they work by making them "citizens" of a "homeland".
* to transfer repressive powers to the "homeland" governments while retaining overall control.
* to gain international acceptance by claiming that South Africa is in fact leading the Namibian "peoples" towards independence.

THE REALITY OF THE "HOMELANDS"

Under the Odendaal Plan, the white area covers some 50.6 million hectares of best farming and government land, townships, diamond areas, native reserves and game parks. This is just under two-thirds of the total land area of Namibia. It contains virtually all Namibia's known base mineral deposits, diamond reserves and the bulk of the commercially active agricultural and fishing sectors. The 32.8 million hectares allocated to the black population vary from thinly-populated semi-desert reserves to highly populated areas such as Ovamboland.[2]

The Odendaal Report admitted that at least one half of the "homelands" could not be made economically viable. For example, though some "homeland" areas have heavy rainfall, the sandy soil cannot retain water, which makes crop cultivation difficult. Ovamboland is 50% without water, Kavangoland 70%.[3]

The "homelands" are dependent on small-scale agriculture but available grazing land is minimal. For example, the area designated as Ovamboland, which contains 40% of the entire Namibian population, comprises only 7% of the territory's land area of which 50% is useful for grazing.[4] Soil erosion resulting from overgrazing forces the African population crowded into these unproductive areas to work in the white economy in order to support themselves.

THE "BANTUSTAN CITIZENS"

South Africa's division of Namibia into "ethnic groups" is arbitrary and denies the development of a national identity. The invention of entities such as "Eastern Caprivi", "Okavangoland" and "Ovamboland" ignores the common historical roots of the population in the north. Many "citizens" do not live in their designated "homeland" and have little or no connection with it. South African statistics, which have frequently been revised in the light of international concern over the territory and are thus suspect, give the following picture:

Population Group	Number		Percentage of total population		Percentage of each group living in their "homeland"
	1970	1974	1970	1974	1970
Ovambos	352,640	396,000	46.3	46.5	83%
Whites	90,583	99,000	11.9	11.6	—
Damaras	66,291	75,000	8.7	8.8	12%
Hereros	50,589	56,000	6.6	6.6	58%
Kavangos	49,512	56,000	6.5	6.6	96%
Namas	32,935	37,000	4.3	4.3	6.6%*
Coloureds	28,512	32,000	3.7	3.8	—
East Caprivians	25,580	29,000	3.3	3.4	98%
Bushmen	22,830	26,000	3.0	3.0	30%
Rehoboth Basters	16,649	19,000	2.2	2.2	79%*
Kaokolanders	6,567	7,000	0.9	0.8	96%
Tswanas	4,407	5,000	0.6	0.6	19%
Other	15,089	15,000	2.0	1.8	—
Total	762,184	852,000	100.0	100.0	—

Sources and notes: The population figures for 1970 and 1974 are taken from the South West Africa Survey 1974, published by the South African Department of Foreign Affairs. Those for 1970 are derived from the South African government's Population Census of 6 May 1970 and those for 1974 are official estimates.

The figures showing the percentage of each "population group" living in its respective "homeland" are derived from information in *Homelands—the Role of the Corporations,* a promotional publication for the South African Bantu Investment Corporation, Chris van Rensburg Publications (Pty) Ltd. p.33. Those marked * are taken from the Odendaal Report, Pretoria, 1964. The other groups have not been allocated an area as a "homeland".

Equally important is the overall distribution of the population. 67% of whites and 14% of Africans (excluding those classified as "Coloured") live in urban areas, where the major concentration of white-owned industry and finance is located.[5] Africans living permanently in the homelands are mostly women, children and old people rejected by the white economy. 90% of African women live in the rural areas, compared to 52% Rehoboth Baster women, and 26.5% Coloured women. Only 24.7% of white women live in the rural areas.[6]

THE BANTUSTAN GOVERNMENTS

Although South Africa now claims to have abandoned its policy of separate development (see Ch. XIII) it has in fact continued to establish tribally-based "governments" in the "homelands". These have been promoted most strongly in the northern part of Namibia, where South African efforts to counter the increasing guerilla activities of SWAPO are concentrated.

Ovamboland elections in 1973 to return a homeland Legislative Assembly took place under a state of emergency declared in 1972 following a general strike, and were boycotted by 97% of the population after a SWAPO campaign. Hundreds of people, among them many SWAPO supporters, were arrested, and SWAPO was prevented from holding meetings.

"Homeland governments" have also been set up in other "homelands" such as Kavango, which became a self-governing area in 1973. Elections took place in Eastern Caprivi in July 1976, an Advisory Board for Bushmen was established in October 1976, in July 1977 a Damara Representative Authority was instituted and the Nama, who had not been allocated a "homeland" by the Odendaal Commission, were given an area in 1972 and a Nama Advisory Council with purely advisory functions was set up in July 1976.

A Chiefs' Council was established as the executive government of the Rehoboth Basters in May 1976, and, following a dispute in the 1977 elections, new elections took place in July 1979.

Negotiations for a Tswana Council took place in early 1977.[7] Meetings with Herero leaders to discuss the creation of a Herero Legislative Assembly stalled in May 1977.[8] Elections for a Coloured Council were held in 1972 and 1974. While no "homeland" was designated for the Coloured people in the Odendaal Plan, discussions have taken place in recent years about granting them their own separate farming region.[9]

In October 1979, it was decided to extend the terms of office of various existing legislative authorities to 31 July 1980, while proposals were being prepared to further implement the "homelands" policy under a new guise. (See Ch. XIII, *Bantustans with a new name*).

V Apartheid in Practice

EDUCATION

Education for blacks in Namibia is based on the premise that they are to be trained for the subservient jobs allocated to them by the white economy. The *Bantu Education Act* of 1953 (No. 47) of South Africa was only applied to Namibia in 1970, but discrimatory education policies have long been implemented.

Education is compulsory for whites, but not for Africans or Coloured people, who are allocated to different schools on an ethnic basis. There is a high drop-out rate among African pupils; 75% fail to complete the first three years primary education, and 97.87% leave before Standard 6. While 68% of white children go to secondary school and further, only 1% of African children reach the first form of secondary school.[1] There are only 32 high schools to absorb the flow from 553 primary schools.[2] The ratio of teachers to pupils in African schools is 1:45, nearly $2\frac{1}{2}$ times as much as for whites. Almost one half of the African teachers have themselves not completed secondary education.[3]

Racial discrimination is also evident in the amount spent on education for the different races. In 1975, R68 was spent per black pupil, compared to R614 per white pupil.[4]

Frequent student protests have occurred against this system. In 1973, for example, primary and high school pupils demonstrated in Damaraland, Ovamboland and Windhoek, and in 1976 students throughout Namibia boycotted classes and exams in protest against bantu education. In October and November 1977, 92 students were expelled from a school for holding a public meeting and 18 from another for possessing SWAPO membership cards.[5]

As part of South Africa's proclaimed intention to remove racial discrimination (see Ch. XIII) bantu education is due to be abolished, but little has been done in practice. In July 1979, plans to establish a South West Africa Examination Board were announced which would prepare a country-wide non-discriminatory educational plan.[6]

HEALTH FACILITIES

Black Namibians have a lower life expectancy, are more prone to disease and have a higher rate of infant mortality than whites. Their health is affected by their poor socio-economic position, and by the discriminatory health-care system.

There are state aided municipal hospitals mainly for whites, subsidized by the illegal South African administration, and mission hospitals, government hospitals

19

and clinics for blacks. Most health-care facilities are concentrated in the towns where the majority of whites live. In the "homelands," where living conditions are in any case poor, there are few clinics and doctors,. For example, in 1977 there were 142 hospital beds in Damaraland, 10 medical practitioners, all white, no dentists, and 16 nurses and midwives, 13 of whom were black.[7] The population of Damaraland was 12,362 in 1970 according to South African sources.[8]

Health expenditure varies sharply according to race. In 1974, the Health Budget of the South African Ministry for Bantu Administration and Development allocated R7.8 per head for the health care of the black population in Namibia, compared with R112 per head for whites.[9]

In 1973, there was one hospital bed for every 72 whites and one for every 143 blacks. In the case of nurses, there was one white nurse for every 125 whites and one black nurse for every 550 blacks. These figures do not take into account the inferior nature of facilities in African clinics.[10]

Levels of life expectancy also differ according to race. Life expectancy among the Ovambos at the end of the 1960's was 33 years for women and 31 for men, compared to 72 years for white women and 65 for white men.[11]

Infant mortality rates reflect the different living standards. In 1975, a Windhoek survey gave a rate of 163 per 1,000 born infants for blacks, 145 for Coloureds and 21 for whites.[12]

HOUSING

Housing conditions in Namibia have been governed by discriminatory laws such as the *Native Urban Areas Proclamation* of 1951, which regulates African residence in urban areas. Although sections of this Proclamation were amended in 1977 to allow Africans for the first time to buy land in urban areas and seek loans from building societies, in practice very few Africans can afford to do so.

In the urban areas, special townships such as Katutura near Windhoek are set aside for black habitation. The old Ovambo hostel in Katutura, which was demolished in September 1978, accommodated about 2,000 contract workers in extremely overcrowded conditions, with 20 men to one room. Sanitary conditions were described as "disgusting, it was cold, damp and sparsely furnished, with a metal box with wooden covers serving as a bed and storage place."[13] The new hostel for about 5,200 contract workers, which was opened in 1978, has better facilities but retains all the worst features of the old system such as providing room only for single men, lacking privacy, and having rooms with high walls and small windows.[14]

A recent report showed alarm at the housing shortage in Khomasdal, residential area for Coloureds. A waiting list had 520 family units on it. Squatter camps were emerging, and the Windhoek City Council admitted that, given the high rate of unemployment, many people without adequate housing could not even afford cheap rented homes.[15] According to another report, Katutura, with an estimated population of 40,000, is in need of another 6,100 houses in 1980, and a further 15,000 houses by 1985. A new township is being planned nearby to provide high density housing.[16]

Poverty among the African population is most evident in the rural areas, where housing is primitive and lacking in most basic facilities. In the "homelands", overpopulation and the lack of building materials force most Africans to live in shanties or huts built of non-permanent materials such as grasses, clay or poles.

Contract workers on white farms suffer an additional problem of being isolated from their home communities. Houses are often corrugated iron huts accommodating a whole family in one small room, without electric light or running water.[17]

PENSIONS AND SOCIAL SECURITY

Africans have little financial security in their old age. Where pensions exist, they are paid on a discriminatory basis according to race, at a ratio of 4:2:1 to whites, Coloureds and Africans. Elderly people and workers no longer useful to the White economy are made to move to the "homelands" where they survive on tiny pensions. One woman from Windhoek, interviewed in January 1977, highlighted their position:

"Because I am young and strong, I can work for myself even if it is for a very poor salary. But I am very concerned about the old people of Namibia, who have a very raw deal. There are so-called homelands to which the old people have been forced to leave. These old people have been offered a so-called old age home, which is in reality a little corrugated room in this terrible heat of Namibia. We need a permit to visit them in the first place, then we are worried because they don't get their food regularly, although it is only porridge in most cases—most of the time their diet consists only of porridge, we don't even know when they do get this."[18]

Findings by a Committee of the Turnhalle Constitutional Conference in 1975 showed that only about 11.6% of the labour force was eligible for pension schemes. Qualifications for membership require that an employee must fall within a definite age range, must have been in the service of his or her employer for a certain continuous term or must hold the post in a permanent capacity.[19] This invariably excludes contract workers who have no control over the "continuity" of their employment.

REMOVALS

The implementation of South Africa's bantustan policy in Namibia has deeply affected peoples' lives. One particularly brutal consequence has been the removal of black people from their homes in areas designated as white under the policy. According to the Odendaal Plan, 28.67% of the non-white population of the country would be required to move to different areas.[20]

Forced removals have caused much hardship and destruction in Namibia. With the creation of the Nama "homeland" for instance, a total of 35,000 persons had

21

been removed from their homes of Neuhoff, Bondelswartz and Hochanas by the end of 1969, which were declared white areas. About 800 Nama in the Hochanas reserve some 200 km south east of Windhoek defied the removal order, and in 1975 were finally granted permission to stay, though the government refused to give any aid or provide schooling facilities.[21]

About 2,000 Damaras were moved from their homes in Usakos to a new township and 500 to Okombahe in Damaraland.[22]

When Hereros resisted being moved to a semi-desert area in the east of the country, where most of their population had been wiped out by the Germans only 60 years before, the South African authorities threatened to remove their water pumps.[23]

Forced removal also affected the people in the north of Namibia when South Africa decided in 1975/6 to form a "free fire zone" of one kilometre width along the entire 1,600 km long border between Namibia and Angola in response to increased SWAPO activity. The area contained large settlements with missions, schools, clinics, shops and cafes. An extension of the emergency regulations throughout the north in May 1976 provided for compulsory evacuation of these and other facilities. Reports indicated that South African police were carrying out the wholesale destruction of villages and crops, and refugees in southern Angola said houses had been flattened, crops burned or ploughed up.[24] Up to 50,000 civilians were forcibly removed from their homes in northern Namibia.[25]

VI   The Economy

ECONOMIC BENEFITS

Namibia has a dual economy with an extremely wealthy white-owned sector which embraces the territory's most valuable natural resources, and a separate subsistence economy in the "homelands" which have been allocated to black people. This unequal system provides a constant supply of black workers from the "homelands" who must supplement their income with wages earned in the white economy.

Statistical information on the Namibian economy is not published regularly due to the South African policy of aggregating figures on Namibia with those of the Republic itself. Such figures as are released are carefully selected to give the impression that Namibia is an economically unviable territory heavily dependent on South African subsidisation. In fact, South Africa, and numerous overseas investors, reap substantial profits from the exploitation of Namibia's natural resources. This is shown in the gap between Namibia's Gross Domestic Product (GDP), representing the total value of goods and services produced in the territory, and Gross National Product (GNP) representing the total value after foreign payments. It has been estimated that over one third, perhaps as much as half, of Namibia's GDP is creamed off each year by outside interests and that the resulting discrepancy between GDP and GNP has got gradually wider.[1]

The principal sectors of the Namibian economy, mining and fishing, are dominated by overseas multinational corporations. Commercial stock raising, particularly of karakul (Persian lamb), is controlled by whites resident in Namibia. South Africa still absorbs most taxation levied in Namibia, including that derived from companies and from mineral rights, since South Africa retains responsibility for the Department of Customs and Excise under which these duties fall. These cash flows are not credited to Namibia in official South African accounts, thus distorting the budgetary calculations concerning Namibia. If distortions of this kind are corrected, it can be shown that Namibia provides a net cash flow to South Africa.[2]

Half of Namibia's exports are estimated to go to South Africa, providing the Republic with vital raw materials. Other exports from Namibia such as to the United Kingdom, which accounts for an estimated 25% of Namibia's exports, earn trade receipts in South Africa.[3]

The commercial exploitation of Namibia is based on three main activities: mining, coastal fishing and commercial stock raising particularly of karakul pelts.

MINING

The economic life of Namibia is dominated by the mining industry, where all the major companies are foreign owned. The principal minerals exploited are diamonds, copper, lead, tin, uranium and zinc, with diamonds leading in terms of value of production.

For instance in 1972, the rate of investment in Namibia was estimated to be £25 million per annum, and 60% of this was going into mining. The mining industry as a whole provides approximately 60% of Namibia's exports, 50% of the GDP and 70% of "public revenue" through taxation.[4]

The two most important mining companies in Namibia are Consolidated Diamond Mines (CDM) and Tsumeb Corporation. CDM is a South African subsidiary of De Beers which is part of the vast Anglo-American Corporation and has extensive British participation. Tsumeb Corporation is owned by American Metal Climax Inc. (AMAX) and other United States and South African corporations, and mines copper, lead and zinc, silver and cadmium. Between them they control 90% of all mining production in Namibia. Investment in mining has been extremely profitable for foreign companies. For example, from 1970 to 1973, CDM's net profits rose from R33.8 million to R96.5 million per annum.[5]

A major recent development in the mining sector has been the exploitation of uranium on a large scale. This is at present concentrated in the Rössing Mine near Swakopmund which is 60% owned by the Rio Tinto Zinc Corporation (RTZ) of Great Britain. The Rössing Mine is the largest open cast uranium mine in the world.

Prospecting is increasing, with most of the large multinational mining companies involved and reportedly setting up small front companies. 29 of the 35 prospecting grants authorised in 1979 were for uranium.[6]

Prospecting for oil and natural gas is also expanding. A gas find off the Namibian coast in 1979 was described by the government-owned company, South African Oil Exploration Corporation (Soekor) as the most significant yet, and might be used to convert to methanol for use as motor fuel. The company is also stepping up the search for oil along the South African and Namibian coast.[7]

FISHING

Commercial fishing is Namibia's second largest industry and is dominated by eight large South African companies or their affiliates. Most of the produce is canned for export. Much of the catch is processed as fish meal for animal feed, thus depriving the population of a valuable nutritional source.[8]

There are only two harbours, Walvis Bay and Lüderitz. There has been a serious decline in both inshore and deep water catches and profitability, caused by ruthless overfishing. This has resulted in a decline in prosperity in both ports.

South Africa proclaimed a 200-mile fishery zone off the Namibian coast in November 1979, and intends to sell fishing rights inside the zone to other nations. This would add an extra R17 million per year to revenue from fishing. The move was condemned by the UN Council for Namibia, which called the South African action "illegal, null and void", claiming that South Africa merely intends to preserve for its own exploitation and plunder the marine wealth off the coast of Namibia, under the pretence of protecting the marine resources of Namibia from depletion.[9]

FARMING

Farming contributes 20% to Namibia's Gross Domestic Product. Commercial agriculture and stockraising are totally controlled by whites, with Africans employed as shepherds and farm labourers. Over 90% of the value of agricultural output is livestock or livestock products.[10]

In contrast to the mining and fisheries sector, most of the farms belong to farmers resident in Namibia. This is true not only for all the subsistence and cash crop farms in the "homelands", but also for most of the 6,324 farms held by some 5,000 whites, who are almost all German and Afrikaans speaking.[11] Blacks own about 25% of the territory's 9 million head of sheep, cattle and goats.

Most of the white farming is centred round the main towns. Namibia produces about half the world's supply of the luxury karakul pelt. Exports go mostly to the Federal Republic of Germany, France, Japan and the United Kingdom. Export earnings from this source have risen sharply from R59 million in 1978 to an estimated R75 million for 1979. Prices for a pelt moved up from R12.24 in July 1978 to R17.15 a year later.[12] Many white farmers have moved into this lucrative export activity. This has allowed a few Africans to move into the stock rearing sector.

African farmers tend toward producing food crops such as meat, maize, millet and ground nuts. Some of these are exported. The cattle industry is controlled by South Africa, and treated as a residual supplier. In 1972, cattle sales amounted to 583,168 head, almost 75 percent of which were exported to South Africa.[13]

COMMERCE AND FINANCE

There is some engineering and construction work but this is largely in support of the mining sector. There has been little or no attempt to establish a capital goods industry, and the overwhelming majority of Namibian imports are machines and equipment.

Namibia imports 90% of all goods through South Africa, creating a high degree of dependence.[14] There is a thriving consumer goods sector, retailing mainly to the white population. Many of the major stores are outlets of South African chains, for example OK Bazaars.

Some banking and insurance companies have branches in Namibia though there is virtually no extension of credit to Africans. Recently many of the institutions, led by the building societies, have started to pull back to South Africa, thus further hampering access to independent funding for small undertakings.[15]

INTERNATIONAL ACTION TO PROTECT NAMIBIA'S ECONOMY

In 1971, the International Court of Justice stated in an Advisory Opinion that there was an obligation on states to abstain from entering into economic forms of relationships or dealings with South Africa on behalf of Namibia.

In 1974, the UN Council for Namibia, as the *de jure* authority over the territory, enacted Decree No. 1 for the Protection of Natural Resources in Namibia, providing *inter alia* that any licence or concession granted by the government of South Africa was null and void, that any natural resources taken from Namibia without the Council's consent were liable to be seized and forfeited and that any person or corporation contravening the Decree might be held liable to damages by the future government of an independent Namibia.

While the UN has lacked effective power to implement these measures, foreign companies which continue to exploit the territory's natural resources are acting in violation of international law.

VII   The Labour Force

SIZE AND STRUCTURE OF THE WORK FORCE

The Namibian labour force is divided along racial lines by apartheid. Discrimination exists in the work situation, the right to organise, the type of jobs available to different races and the wages they receive.

The total Namibian workforce is estimated at between 500,000—525,000. Of these, 36,500 are whites employed predominantly in large-scale modern agriculture, government service and commerce. They make up 75% of the managerial/administrative and technical professional groups, forming a highly paid elite.[1] Only an estimated 100 Africans and 250 Coloureds came in the managerial/administrative category in 1977.[2]

Of the black workers, an estimated 240,000 work in small-scale or subsistence agriculture and about 75,000 are employed in domestic service. Excluding these two categories, African employment is of the order of 150,000. About one-third of these work in the white-owned agricultural sector, an eighth each in mining and commerce, a tenth in government, just under a tenth in construction and just over one fifteenth in manufacturing and public utilities.

Domestic service and work on white farms provided over 50% of black employment and are the lowest paid jobs.[3]

A minority of workers are permanent residents in the black townships of the Police Zone or on white-owned farms. Most of them are migrant workers. Because the "homelands" are incapable of supporting their population, the majority of black Namibians are forced to migrate, mainly from the northern areas of Ovamboland and Kavangoland, to work for white employers on contracts of up to 30 months at a stretch.[4]

Black workers coming from reserves in the Police Zone, such as the Nama and Hereros, and Coloured people, normally work on 6-12 month contracts. Contract workers are estimated to constitute between one half and three quarters of all black employees in Namibia.[5]

MIGRANT LABOUR

The migrant labour system has created deep resentment in the workers subjected to it. It entails long periods away from their homes while their families have to eke out a living in the homelands, low wages and squalid living conditions in single men's hostels which are often raided by police.

Widespread protests led to a general strike in 1971-2 sparked off by contract workers and supported by SWAPO. This was brutally repressed by South

African police and army, and a state of emergency was declared in Ovamboland on 4 February 1972 (*Proclamation R 17*).

A "new" labour agreement was announced, which did not essentially change any of the harsh conditions of contract labour. The South West Africa Labour Association (SWANLA), the official agency which coordinated the recruiting and transport of contract workers, was abolished, and replaced by a system of labour bureaux operated by the tribal authorities in the "homelands".

All male adults under the age of 65 were required to register with the labour bureaux as work seekers and were obliged to accept the job and wage they were offered. The tribal labour officer would classify job applicants into different employment categories, leaving the worker no choice of his employer or of the wage-rate.

Until October 1977, all Africans were obliged to carry passes and produce them on demand. As in South Africa they could not remain in an urban area longer than 72 hours if they were not employed, unless they had acquired residence rights. A number of these "pass laws" were repealed in October 1977. Africans no longer have to carry passes, and can in theory stay without limit in urban areas while looking for work. In practice, they may not seek, accept or remain in employment without official permission and they must still have their contracts registered. A fine for employers who fail to register their Black employees was raised from R100 to R300 (or 6 months imprisonment) at the same time as the reforms.[6]

UNEMPLOYMENT

Black unemployment is endemic in an economy geared to the needs of a white minority and overseas investors, where new jobs are created at far too slow a rate to absorb population growth. Unemployment among blacks has increased so rapidly recently that a Committee on Labour was established in early 1978 to look into the problem.

One researcher estimated that between 1969 and 1979 the proportion of the black labour force (including subsistence farmers) which fell into the category unemployed/unspecified rose from 11.2% to 13.2%, while those "employed" in subsistence farming increased from 86,000 to 91,000.[7] This latter category conceals many effectively unemployed.

The decision to abolish influx control in October 1977 meant that black workers from the reserves could now more easily search for jobs in white urban areas. This, and the development of the armed struggle in the north, led to a sharp increase in visible unemployment. The Windhoek Town Clerk estimated in February 1978 that between 500 and 1,000 black unemployed were illegally staying in Katutura each night. Unemployment for established black residents of Windhoek had risen from 3% to 12%, he said, and blamed the workers themselves for the hardship they experienced.

Employers were taking advantage by hiring Ovambo workers prepared to work for half the wage.[8] Big employers such as the municipality and railways received between 15 and 80 job applications each day.[9] The task of the Labour Committee was to create work opportunities in towns and cities and in the reserves to encourage work-seekers back to their own areas. One short-term solution was to offer free transport "home".[10] A member of the right wing white Aktur group said in March 1980 that 40,000 unemployed workers were walking the streets. Most of them were in Windhoek.[11]

New measures were being considered in April 1980 to deal with the unemployment problem. These included the registration of both workers and employers, protection against competition from foreign workers and a possibility of a person being declared "idle".[12]

WAGES

Exact wage statistics relating to Namibia are difficult to obtain as the South African authorities do not publish a series of wages or cost-of living data. One survey has estimated that the annual per capita personal income of whites in Namibia is in the region of R3,000 per head per year, while for blacks it is R125 per year—a ratio of 24:1.[13]

Wage levels have in many cases risen considerably since the 1971-72 strike, but are by no means sufficient to meet the needs of black workers and their families.

Racial inequalities persist in most wage payments. For example between 1971 and 1975, wages for black miners at the Tsumeb mine were reported to have almost doubled from an average inclusive wage of US$63.95 per month (of which US$29.70 was paid in cash) to US$120 (US$64 in cash). Average cash wages for white miners had meanwhile risen from US$494.11 per month to about US$750.[14] The lowest African wages are in domestic service (approx. R125-200 per annum) and farmwork (ca. R250-400 per annum including payment in food and shelter); these two sectors employ the large majority of black workers.[15] Gradations exist within the black workforce: contract workers from the North are paid lower wages than local African workers in the Police Zone, the latter are paid less than Coloured and Rehoboth workers, who earn less than white employees. Black women in all categories of work earn less than their male counterparts, and less than white women.[16] For example, in 1978, black nursing sisters earned a minimum of R2,193 per annum, white sisters R3,639.[17]

COST OF LIVING

Namibia has a higher cost of living than South Africa, from where it imports the bulk of its manufactured goods and a large amount of food. Prices vary between different parts of the country; food and other costs in the northern "homelands" maybe 50% higher than in the Windhoek shops.[18]

In October 1976 the household subsistence level (which is an estimate of the amount necessary to afford a family of usually five bare survival) for Coloured families in Windhoek was computed at R176.81 per month and for African at R151.14.[19] Wages remained much lower; one preliminary survey based on information from employers put wages in the farming sector at between R6 and R25 per month; R11 for domestic workers, R40 to R100 in the state electrical industry SWAWEK and R40 to R80 per month in the metal industry.[20]

TRADE UNIONS

Labour relations in Namibia are governed by the *Wages and Industrial Conciliation Ordinance* of 1952, which excludes the largest group of black workers, on farms and in domestic service, from its provisions. Until recently, it did not recognise Africans as "employees", denying African trade unions the right to register. Africans were also excluded from provisions dealing with the right to strike. While it was not illegal for African workers to form and join their own trade unions, such unions could not apply for registration and were not recognised by the authorities for the settlement of disputes. In July 1978 this clause in the Ordinance was abolished.

African workers are now in theory free to join existing white-dominated unions such as the South West Africa Municipal Staff Association (MSA), the Mine Workers Union, the Fishermens' Unions (Coloured and White) at Lüderitz and one or two others. The Municipal Staff Association asked the Department of Labour to re-register it, allowing it to admit some 2,000 black workers, but proposed an amendment as a precautionary measure to prevent white members being outvoted by blacks.[21]

The new legislation of July 1978 contained political restrictions, making it illegal for a registered trade union to affiliate or grant financial assistance to any political party. No trade union is permitted to receive financial assistance from a political party. This seems intended to seriously hinder the activities of the National Union of Namibian Workers (NUNW), a countrywide organisation formed in 1978 and affiliated to the South West Africa People's Organisation (SWAPO) whose aims it shares.

INDUSTRIAL ACTION

Black Namibian workers have a long history of struggle against oppression. In the 20 years from 1950-1971, 43 collective actions by Ovambo contract workers in the white industrial sector were reported in the local press.[22] At the end of 1971, a two month long general strike took place, involving 13,000 migrant workers protesting against the contract labour system and influx control. The strike had wide support among the entire African population. It brought the mining industry to a halt and seriously affected other areas of business. The South African authorities sent in police reinforcements, surrounded the migrant workers' compound at Katutura and repatriated thousands to Ovamboland. In January 1972, the South African Defence Force was sent to Namibia; strike meetings were fired upon and thousands arrested. A state of emergency was declared in Ovamboland which banned all meetings and allowed for wide powers of arrest.

The strike resulted in mainly cosmetic changes in labour recruitment policy, but the greatest effect was the increased militancy and political consciousness of the black population. Industrial unrest has continued since 1972 despite the risks involved for the workers. In November 1976 for example, 700 Damara workers at the Rössing Uranium mine owned by Rio Tinto Zinc walked out following complaints about the poor quality and high cost of all food supplied in the company canteens.[23]

In 1977, Nama teachers throughout the country struck for equal pay with Coloured teachers. The strike continued until January 1978, but was called off in the face of South African intransigence. Strikes took place simultaneously at several mines in January 1979. 2,000 workers at the Rössing mine struck from late December to early January over wage increases and conditions of employment.[24]

More than 200 workers at the Krantzberg tungsten mine near Omaruru were sacked by management for going on strike.

500 workers at the Uis tin mine owned by the South African Iron and Steel Corporation (ISCOR) stopped work over complaints about industrial relations, low wages and general intimidation of workers.[25] In May 1979 the entire black workforce at CDM's diamond mine in Oranjemund struck for 2 days after a lidless, empty container for phosphine tablets, a poisonous substance, was found in a bag of corn meal used by the workers.[26]

Several hundred workers went on strike at the CDM diamond mine in September 1979, following a dispute about working hours.[27]

VIII   The Denial of Human Rights

REPRESSIVE LAWS

The instruments of repression used by South Africa in Namibia are largely the same as those used in the Republic. They are applied almost exclusively against the black population and those whites who support the liberation movement.

They remain in existence despite South Africa's claim to be leading Namibia towards independence, and new repressive legislation has been enacted to counter the growing impact of the liberation struggle.

The *Internal Security Amendment Act* of 1976 embodies the provisions of the *Suppression of Communism Act* 1950 which was extended to Namibia in 1966 and made retrospective, and the *Riotous Assembly Act* 1956 which was extended to Namibia in 1976. It allows for the banning of organisations and the prohibition of gatherings and other political activities. While SWAPO has not yet been banned, its members have suffered constant harrassment and frequent detention, forcing the movement virtually underground by 1979.

The *Terrorism Act* of 1967, made retrospective to 1962 to allow for the trial of 37 SWAPO members, has been used against political activists. It provides for the death penalty for a wide definition of "terroristic activities" such as the "intent to endanger the maintenance of law and order". It empowers any high ranking police officer to arrest any person suspected of being or having aided a "terrorist" and provides for indefinite detention of people for interrogation.

Proclamation AG26 of April 1978 reinforces these measures, empowering the police to detain, for indefinite periods, any person considered to constitute a threat to the peaceful political process in Namibia. Detainees have no recourse to the courts. This law has been used to detain a large number of SWAPO members and supporters. *Proclamation AG50* of 1978 allows for the deportation of persons considered to be a threat to good government. This was used to deport a number of people, among them church leaders, who were critical of the internal elections in December 1978. (See Ch. XIII).

EMERGENCY REGULATIONS

Although the emergency regulations in force in Ovamboland since 1972 and extended to the whole of northern Namibia in 1976 were repealed in November 1977, they were replaced by new measures which maintain virtual martial law over large areas of the country.

Under *Proclamation AG9* of November 1977, any area can be declared a security district. The Proclamation has been amended several times, subjecting

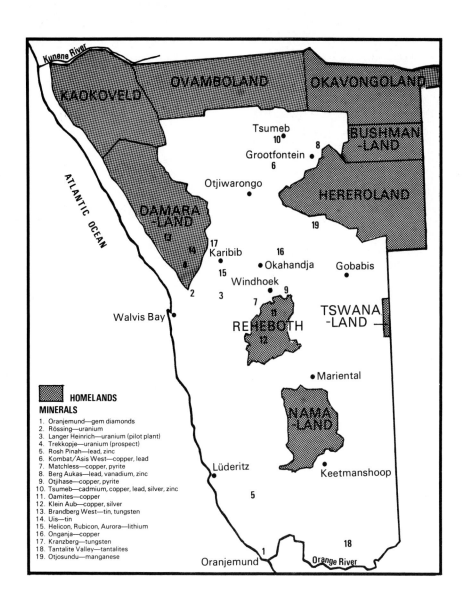

MINERALS

1. Oranjemund—gem diamonds
2. Rössing—uranium
3. Langer Heinrich—uranium (pilot plant)
4. Trekkopje—uranium (prospect)
5. Rosh Pinah—lead, zinc
6. Kombat/Asis West—copper, lead
7. Matchless—copper, pyrite
8. Berg Aukas—lead, vanadium, zinc
9. Otjihase—copper, pyrite
10. Tsumeb—cadmium, copper, lead, silver, zinc
11. Oamites—copper
12. Klein Aub—copper, silver
13. Brandberg West—tin, tungsten
14. Uis—tin
15. Helicon, Rubicon, Aurora—lithium
16. Onganja—copper
17. Kranzberg—tungsten
18. Tantalite Valley—tantalites
19. Otjosundu—manganese

Advertisements from commercial magazines in Namibia

Copper from Tsumeb Mine awaiting shipment, Walvis Bay   Photo: *Kimmo Kiljunen*

Katatura Township, Windhoek   *Photo: Kimmo Kiljunen*

School in Elin Village, Ovamboland   *Photo: Kimmo Kiljunen*

Namibians taken prisoner by German troops during the early colonial period

Victims of early German colonial policies of starvation and genocide

Photo: Komitee Zuidelijk Afrika, Amsterdam

Prisoners taken by South African troops during raids into Angola, May 1978

Victims of South African attack on Kassinga Refugee camp

South African troops returning from a strike into Angola

Results of South African attacks on a factory inside Angola

Workers at Oranjemund diamond field   Photo: *Gavin Shreeve*

Workers transport, Windhoek   Photo: *Kimmo Kiljunen*

Sam Nujoma — President of SWAPO

PLAN troops

effectively 50% of the territory and 80% of the population to a form of martial law and even affecting areas such as Windhoek. It gives police powers to search, arrest, question and detain people for up to 30 days. Its provisions have been strengthened particularly in Ovamboland where the South African army faces growing guerilla fighting. A dusk to dawn curfew was imposed on Ovamboland in June 1979, prohibiting anyone to travel at night without permission.[1]

New security measures were introduced by the Administrator General on 18 July 1979, declaring the entire north of Namibia a restricted area for civilian aircraft. It means among other things that no civilian aircraft may fly in the restricted area between 6 p.m. and 6 a.m., or fly below 3000 feet above ground level. Security forces also introduced a convoy system in the north, supplying armed escorts for motorists on certain routes.[2]

An amendment to *Proclamation AG9* was introduced on 6 February 1980, giving the Officer Commanding the South African Defence Force or his representatives powers to prohibit travel on any road in Ovamboland at times they may specify, or without such escort as the security forces may provide. It also prohibits any person selling any merchandise from dusk to dawn in Ovamboland without the consent of these authorities (*Government Notice AG8, 6.2.80*).

New security measures were also introduced in Kaokoland, which borders on Ovamboland, after an admission by the South African Defence Force that SWAPO guerillas were active there.

Kaokoland is not officially part of the "operational area". In a Proclamation promulgated on 19 December 1979, *(Proclamation AG119)* Sections 3, 4 and 5 of *Proclamation AG9* were extended to Kaokoland. These empower the Administrator General to control or direct people's movement in the affected area, and to declare any security district along the international border of Namibia a "prohibited area". They also empower the South African military forces to search, arrest and detain people without a warrant, and stipulate 24 hours notice to the authorities about any meeting.

MASS ARRESTS

The South African security forces have increasingly resorted to large-scale arrests as a means of silencing growing opposition to the regime's control over Namibia. Harrassment and detention has particularly affected members and supporters of the liberation movement SWAPO. The entire leadership of SWAPO inside Namibia has periodically been imprisoned.

Several hundred people were arrested in 1973 in the aftermath of a boycott of the Ovamboland elections, which took place while emergency regulations were in force there (see Ch. IV). In November 1973, 105 SWAPO members were arrested from all parts of the country and held in solitary confinement. SWAPO had been the primary target of police repression in 1975/76 because of its opposition to the Windhoek constitutional talks then in progress.[3]

33

The installation of an Administrator General in Namibia in 1977 was ostensibly to prepare for free elections with full participation of all political forces. In fact, it heralded even greater measures of repression, while South Africa prepared to impose its own internal solution on Namibia. More than 70 SWAPO officials and members were arrested in April 1979[4] and the SWAPO offices in Windhoek had to close down for fear of further arrests. In June 1979, some 5,000 people were arrested in Katutura township.[5] These arrests were described by the South African police as having no political implications, but township residents said police and troops were looking for "terrorists".[6]

DETENTION WITHOUT TRIAL

The *Terrorism Act* of 1967 and *Proclamation AG26* of April 1978 have been freely used by the South African regime to keep detainees in prison without trial for long periods. Many of the hundreds of people arrested after the assassination of the Ovambo Chief Minister Elifas in 1975 spent three months or more in detention before being released without having been charged.[7]

Most of SWAPO's internal leadership has suffered periodic detention for long periods. Axel Johannes, the Administrative Secretary of SWAPO has spent the last seven years in and out of police custody.[8] In 1974, he spent five months in solitary confinement under the *Terrorism Act*. In August 1975, he was detained incommunicado for five months before being sentenced to one year's imprisonment for refusing to give evidence in the trial of six SWAPO members. In 1977, he was detained twice for several months, and again in 1978. He was among those detained under *Proclamation AG26* in April 1979. He has repeatedly suffered severe torture.[9]

Of 200 prisoners taken by the South African forces during their bombing raid on Kassinga refugee camp in southern Angola in May 1978, 137 have been detained incommunicado, without charge or trial, apparently under the *Terrorism Act*.[10]

South Africa has persistently blocked moves to send a group of international lawyers to Namibia to investigate the fate of the Kassinga detainees and that of other people reported to have disappeared.

BANNINGS

Banning orders have been used in Namibia to silence South Africa's opponents. In January 1980, the regime began releasing a number of the detainees held under *Proclamation AG26*. They were, however, placed under severe restrictions amounting to banning orders, preventing them from carrying out any political activities. They are restricted to a stipulated municipal town or area, prohibited from attending meetings of more than five people, restricted from receiving visitors and restricted in their movements from sunrise to sunset.[11]

Detentions without trial continue, however, as part of the general harrassment of SWAPO supporters and other opponents. SWAPO offices in Windhoek have been periodically raided and the workers detained, as happened for instance on 7 February 1980.[12]

POLITICAL PRISONERS

Political activists in Namibia are frequently convicted for "crimes" such as addressing rallies and organising boycotts, which elsewhere are part of the normal political process. Under the *Terrorism Act* and the *Sabotage Act* imposed by South Africa such activities are interpreted as inciting people to violence or helping "terrorist activities". According to the South African Prisons Department, 53 Namibian political prisoners were held on Robben Island in March 1980. Many more are held in other prisons in South Africa and Namibia, although their whereabouts is often unknown. Almost all of these convicted political prisoners are members or supporters of SWAPO. The majority have been tried under the *Terrorism Act* by South African-established courts in Namibia.

In 1968, Herman ja Toivo, SWAPO's most eminent founder member, was sentenced to 20 years imprisonment under the *Terrorism Act*, together with 36 SWAPO members convicted at the same trial. 19 received life sentences and are on Robben Island.[13] (See Appendix for Toivo's statement in Court).

In 1974, three SWAPO Youth League members were sentenced to eight years imprisonment under the *Sabotage Act* for addressing a public rally in Windhoek in August 1973 , and in a separate trial the former Chairman of SWAPO's Youth League received a 6 year sentence.[14]

In 1976, worldwide attention was focused on the trial of Aaron Muchimba, SWAPO's national organiser, Hendrik Shikongo and four other SWAPO members who were charged under the *Terrorism Act* in connection with the assassination in April 1975 of Chief Elifas of Ovamboland. None of the six SWAPO members was accused of the murder of Chief Elifas. Hendrik Shikongo was charged with having transported three men to the scene of the murder. The others were accused of giving sums of cash and other forms of material support to alleged "terrorists".

Muchimba and Shikongo were sentenced to death in May 1976, the first death sentences imposed under the Act.[15] Two others, Ms Rauna Nambinga and Ms Anna Nghihondjwa, were sentenced to seven and five years imprisonment respectively. Following international protests, an appeal was allowed which showed up serious irregularities in the trial proceedings. Information relating to the defence had been passed on to the security police in the course of the trial. The sentences were set aside by the Appellate Division of the Bloemfontein Supreme Court on 17 May 1977, and the prisoners were released.[16]

In November 1978, two SWAPO members on trial for allegedly sabotaging bridges were sentenced to 18 years imprisonment, a third to six years. All were tried under the *Terrorism Act*.[17] Earlier that year one man was sentenced to 13 years for encouraging or inciting civilians to undergo training in counter-insurgency,[18] another received an eight-year sentence for "participating in terroristic activities".[19] A third was sentenced to eight years imprisonment for "supplying goods to terrorists".[20]

TORTURE

Detailed evidence exists that torture is used commonly and routinely on Namibian political prisoners and detainees.

In May 1977, Lutheran, Anglican and Roman Catholic church leaders in Namibia signed a statement pointing out that electric shock, burning with cigarettes and sleep deprivation were apparently standard police procedure.[21]

Eyewitness accounts were given by former detainees of brutality and torture at the notorious military internment camp in Oshakati (Ovamboland). One secondary school student was tortured there for five days in December 1976 with electric shock, beaten while he was blindfolded, and tied to a pole in the open for several hours.[22] One pregnant woman was tortured in a similar way and died as a result.[23] Virtually every South African military base has an internment centre attached to it.

A paper prepared by a Catholic pastor in November 1976, which resulted in his expulsion, stated that inhuman treatment, both physical and psychological, was taking place throughout Namibia, and listed eight places where torture was practised.[24] Such allegations have repeatedly been denied by the authorities in Namibia, but evidence shows that the practice continues. According to eye-witness accounts of released detainees, a number of the prisoners held at a camp at Hardap Dam near Mariental, who were captured during the Kassinga raid in 1978, have been subjected to physical maiming, having their eyes and ears removed and limbs severed from their bodies.[25]

In January 1980, Lucia Hamutenya, SWAPO Secretary for Legal Affairs, gave details of reports of torture she had collected from victims in Namibia. These included dropping victims from helicopters, applying electric shock torture and sexual assaults on women.[26]

FLOGGING

In September 1973, following the successful boycott of the Ovambo elections, a new form of reprisal was used. Men and women thought to be political opponents were subjected to public floggings by the Ovambo tribal authorities. They were not tried in any court of law but simply handed over to the tribal chiefs by the South African security police on the basis of unsubstantiated allegations. Between 1973 and 1975, several hundred Ovambos were subjected to floggings; often sentences of up to 30 lashes were imposed by "tribal courts" without any explanations.

36

Floggings were carried out with a branch from a palm tree, inflicting severe injuries. Many victims suffered lasting ill-health as a result.[27] As a result of the international outcry provoked by such methods, and court action brought by Anglican and Lutheran church leaders, the Ovambo tribal authorities were forced to discontinue flogging in public in 1975.

PRISON CONDITIONS

Namibian detainees are held in prisons and open air detention centres throughout the country. Prisons are reportedly extremely overcrowded, particularly during the periods of mass arrests.[28] While police refuse to reveal the location of detention centres, some 18 camps are known to exist.

Released detainees have described the appalling conditions they have suffered. Generally, food is bad and inadequate. South African authorities frequently deprive political prisoners of food and water to force them to give information.[29] Sanitary conditions are described as intolerable.[30]

In Onuno detention camp in the north, people were huddled together in a fenced enclosure without a roof over their heads and without blankets. Each had to put a bag over his head during the day so as not to see what was happening in the military camp to which the detention camp is attached. Rations consisted of one tin of beans and one can of water per day.[31]

At Ondangua, prisoners have been kept in a corrugated iron stall, with 10 to 11 men in a room 3.5 metres by 3 metres in size, because the main gaol was overcrowded.[32]

Detention sheds at Oshikango consist of corrugated iron huts so constructed that those confined were unable to stand up. Up to six people were held at a time, often for over a week, before being transferred to the detention centre at Oshikati.[33]

One released detainee, describing conditions at Windhoek gaol in 1974, said that whenever he passed from one room to another, someone was at the door to hit him; this was a general feature of the gaol. Food was given twice a day, breakfast at 7 a.m. consisting of maize porridge with mustard and tea, and lunch at 4 p.m., also maize. No relative or other visitors were allowed.[34]

At Hardap Dam, near Mariental in the south of Namibia, inmates are required to do hard labour such as digging roads and felling trees, and widespread torture is evident.[35]

ROBBEN ISLAND

Many Namibian political prisoners are kept more than a thousand miles from their home in South Africa's maximum security prison on Robben Island. According to the South African Minister of Prisons, there were 53 Namibians on Robben Island in March 1980.[36]

Letters which have been smuggled out in 1970 and 1976 speak of terrible conditions there. Prisoners are forced to carry out hard labour at the lime quarries and to gather, process and pack seaweed. Both activities expose them to serious health hazards. Food consists mainly of mealie meal porridge with a tiny piece of fish or meat.

Namibian prisoners can expect few visitors. Fear of harrassment, a complex bureaucracy which requires permission from a number of authorities, and the cost of such a trip have made visits a difficult undertaking. Letters are censored and take months to arrive there.

Namibian prisoners as a group are kept separate from other prisoners, thus increasing their isolation.[37] Prisoners are forbidden any newspapers or radio and many books and magazines. Study is restricted and discouraged. Post-matric studies are no longer allowed. According to Ms. Helen Suzman, an opposition M.P. in the South African Parliament who spoke to Herman ja Toivo during a visit to Robben Island in May 1980, Namibian prisoners lack funds to further their studies.[38] A divide and rule policy is imposed which tries to promote conflict among African and Coloured prisoners and among different "categories" by giving different diets and allowing some prisoners certain privileges while withholding them from others.

Medical care is inadequate, often prisoners are given the wrong medicine or receive no medical attention. Tuberculosis seems prevalent, no doubt aggravated by the bad living conditions and poor diet. There is daily brutality from the authorities, assaults from warders and punishment in isolation cells with reduced diet.[39]

"AMNESTY" OFFER

In December 1979, SWAPO guerillas were offered an "amnesty" if they surrendered to the security forces. The arrangement was hedged about with so many qualifications that it amounted to little more than a call to surrender, and was condemned by SWAPO. Under the "amnesty", guerillas who gave themselves up were to be given an "indemnity certificate", kept for 30 days in detention for purposes of identification and health measures, and then reintegrated with civilian life. An elaborate propaganda campaign to induce SWAPO guerillas to surrender involved setting up two "reception points" to deal with the expected influx, the appointment of an "amnesty officer", distribution of pamphlets and broadcasts into neighbouring Angola. The amnesty period was initially due to expire on 30 April 1980, but was later extended to the end of August. Only four people were reported to have given themselves up by the time the first deadline expired.[40] Calls by SWAPO and groups such as the Namibia National Front and SWAPO Democrats for the release of detainees and political prisoners in Namibia were rejected by the Administrator General. As such, the exercise was shown to be simply a publicity stunt with very little success.

IX Control of the Press and the Media

The only African-controlled newspapers in Namibia are the Lutheran Church organ *Omaweto* (The Friend), and SWAPO's publication *Ombuzeya Namibia*, which circulates clandestinely and is published irregularly because of the constant harrassment of SWAPO members. Both appear in local languages. The rest of the press serves the Afrikaans, English and German speaking communities and is aligned with the political positions of the different white parties.

The *Windhoek Advertiser*, a daily paper which had given some space to political statements from black organisations, was taken over in April 1978 by a West German publishing firm and brought into line with the political aspirations of Dirk Mudge, the white leader of the Democratic Turnhalle Alliance (DTA). The newspaper served as an election vehicle for the DTA in the internal elections of December 1978.[1] (See Ch. XIII, *Internal Elections*). There were rumours of South African funds being channelled into taking over the *Windhoek Advertiser* and another paper, the *Allgemeine Zeitung*, both of whose editors were sacked.[2]

South Africa imposed total control on the media during the December 1978 internal elections, offering free trips to foreign journalists and public figures.[3] The DTA used buses equipped with TV sets in a massive propaganda campaign.[4]

Evidence of official censorship was given by the *Windhoek Observer*, a weekly paper which follows a more open-minded editorial policy than the other papers. In May 1979, its front page, which was to have carried a story about a secret military project, was censored on instruction from South Africa's military commander in Namibia.[5] In October 1979, a four page special supplement about SWAPO's military strategy was banned by the security police.[6]

In November 1979, two Swiss journalists were refused an extension of their work permits in Namibia because they had tried to investigate a "sensitive area". In an interview one of the journalists said she believed this referred to allegations of SWAPO prisoners being kept at Mariental detention camp after the Kassinga massacre by the South African Defence Force.[7]

The SWA Broadcasting Corporation, established in May 1979, is under direct supervision of the Administrator General.[8] South African programmes predominate, though the local content has been increased. The BBC and several West German radio stations are completing negotiations to provide programmes.[9] The SWA Broadcasting Corporation aims to clamp down on "pirate listening" and to compile a listeners' register, clearly to suppress SWAPO's radio broadcasts beamed to Namibia from Zambia and Angola.[10]

The installation of television has been planned since 1972 but little progress has been made yet.

X The Church

MISSIONARIES

Christian missionaries were among the first whites to establish contact with the indigenous people of Namibia. The London and Wesleyan Missionary Societies worked among the Namas, Damaras and Hereros in the southern sector, transferring their work to the Rhenish Missionary Society (RMG) in 1842, which extended its influence among the Rehoboth Basters when they settled in Namibia in the 1870s. The Finnish Mission established itself among the Ovambos around that time, the Catholic Mission arrived in the Okavango in 1910 and the Seventh Day Adventists in Eastern Caprivi in 1920.[1] Anglican missionary activity was extended on a regular basis to Namibia in 1916.

Early missionary endeavours took the form of rudimentary education geared mainly to the work of christianisation, and mission schools concentrated on bible-reading. Some basic hygiene and medical care were also introduced.

Christianity rapidly became the mass religion of all sections of Namibian society as, in the wake of military defeat, Africans flocked to the churches. This came to have a profound effect on the direction of the early struggle for independence and on the churches' later political stand.

AFRICANISATION OF THE CHURCHES

The 1940s and 1950s saw a growing drive in the churches for autonomy from European-based missionary societies. The RMG was succeeded by the Evangelical Lutheran Church, which now has about 130,000 members and is almost completely black. The Evangelical Lutheran OvamboKavango Church, successor to the Finnish Mission, has over 280,000 members, mainly black. The two churches entered into a federal structure known as the United Evangelical Lutheran Church of SWA (UELC) in 1972, and together hold a membership of more than one third of Namibia's population.[2] The majority of the Anglican Church's 60,000 members are African, and similarly the 100,000 members of the Catholic Church.

POLITICISATION OF THE CHURCH

Individual clergy have condemned the oppression of black people in Namibia for many years. However, in the past, their churches restricted themselves largely to their pastoral and diaconal activities. The Lutheran churches, according to one member, took over the tradition of loyalty to the State which became often uncritical and submissive obedience.[3]

As the implementation of apartheid policies progressed in Namibia, the churches came to play an increasingly significant role as the moral conscience of Namibia, and contributed to drawing international attention to violations of human rights in the territory. Members of the Lutheran and African churches were also active in the liberation movement, and prominent church leaders such as the Anglican Bishop Colin Winter supported the aims of the liberation struggle.

This political role was spelt out at the Conference of the United Evangelical Lutheran Church in 1974, which asserted that "the gospel has political consequences. It is thus difficult to preach the message of peace and reconciliation when the opposite is witnessed by society."[4]

CHURCH PROTESTS AGAINST APARTHEID

In 1971, the Lutheran churches submitted an Open Letter to the South African Prime Minister in which they condemned the intimidation and humiliation suffered by black people, demanded the total abolition of apartheid and stressed the integrity of Namibia as one nation. The Anglican Bishop of Damaraland and the Roman Catholic Church gave public support to the letter.

Since the Open Letter, the Anglican and Lutheran churches, with growing support from the Roman Catholic and Methodist churches, have made a number of representations to the South African government against violations of human rights. For example, Bishop Colin Winter gave outspoken support to the nationwide 1971/2 strike and was subsequently expelled from Namibia. In 1973, members of SWAPO, who included pastors, evangelists and members of the church, were intimidated and tortured for resistance to the Ovamboland elections. In 1972/3 Anglican and Lutheran church leaders took legal action against the public floggings of hundreds of Namibians. The new Anglican Bishop Richard Wood was expelled in 1975 for his part in the protest.

In May 1979, the Namibian Council of Churches, formed in October 1978 by the Lutheran, the Anglican, the Congregational and the Methodist church, expressed its concern and dismay over the mass detentions of Namibian citizens under *Proclamation AG26* to the Administrator General in an Open Letter.[5]

Church leaders have suffered frequent harrassment by the South African authorities. The printing press, bookshop and office of the OvamboKavango Lutheran Church organ, *The Friend,* were burnt to the ground in 1973.[6] An Anglican and a Roman Catholic priest were expelled in July 1978 because of their critical attitude to South Africa's brutal treatment of Namibians,[7] in August 1979, Archdeacon Shilongo, the most senior Anglican churchman in the north of Namibia, was arrested at an Anglican mission for having "SWAPO propaganda material" on the premises.[8]

THE CHURCH, POLITICAL PARTIES AND
THE ISSUE OF VIOLENCE

There are political and theological debates within the churches about involvement in political parties and the question of violence.

The Lutheran churches oppose apartheid and oppression because they see these as conflicting with the will of God and the Bible. Within these churches, many younger men favour closer identification with political movements struggling for independence; some older ministers and missionaries oppose this, while the majority accepts the need for political activity but forbids church members from entering party politics. The leader of the Evangelical Lutheran Church sees the role of the church as that of a mediator, and the United Lutheran Church played an important part in promoting the Namibian National Convention—a coalition of groups opposed to the Turnhalle Constitutional Conference. (see Ch. XI, *Solidarity against apartheid*) The Rev. Kameeta, a prominent theologian and SWAPO member, was elected as its President in January 1976. While the Lutheran churches have not condemned armed struggle, they preach the Gospel of reconciliation and the path of non-violent resistance as a positive action which could, in the last resort, mean the overthrow of structures which are against the will of God.[9]

Some white representatives of the Anglican Church in Namibia, such as Bishops Winter and Woods, will speak in support of SWAPO and, while not themselves engaged in violent struggle, accept its necessity.

XI Political Groupings

THE POLITICAL SPECTRUM

Political organisation in Namibia centres around the different paths envisaged for the country's future. The entrenched white power structure has been increasingly challenged by a successful liberation movement uniting those who are opposed to the attempts at a South African imposed settlement. The middle ground is occupied by groups who, while opposed to apartheid, also seek to discredit SWAPO, which has mass support both in the country and internationally, and claim to be acting as a balancing factor between SWAPO and the white political parties.

The different political positions were crystallized in the activities before, during and after the Constitutional Conference of the Turnhalle, which claimed to discuss steps for genuine Namibian independence while drawing its representatives from South African promoted tribal groupings based on the bantustan model. (For Turnhalle proceedings, see Ch. XIII).

The divisions among political groups reflect the divide and rule policy of South Africa, though an increasing number of groups have allied themselves with SWAPO. The emergence of a "centrist" alliance objectively serves South African interest which is to exclude SWAPO from any political settlement. Such groups can be presented as alternatives to SWAPO or at least as deserving equal weight.

ORIGINS OF ORGANISED PROTEST

Opposition to colonialism emerged in the 1940s and 1950s through several strands of activity. Traditional leaders such as the Herero Chief Hosea Kutako and the Nama Chief David Witbooi submitted numerous petitions for Namibian independence to the United Nations. Namibian students in South Africa formed the SWA Student Body which worked closely with the Herero Chiefs Council. The Namibian contract workers provided the strongest base for the future national liberation movement, beginning with the formation of the Ovamboland Peoples Congress in Cape Town in 1957, renamed the **Ovamboland People's Organisation (O.P.O.)** a year later. Its immediate aim was to protest against the conditions of contract workers.

Herman Ja Toivo was instrumental in its formation and, after being expelled from South Africa, worked tirelessly in Ovamboland to gain support. In April 1959, OPO was launched in Windhoek. Later that year, on 10 December 1959, protesters against forced removals from the old location of Windhoek were brutally attacked by the police who killed 11 and wounded 54 and arrested, banned or restricted most of the nationalist leaders. The event contributed to a recognition of the need for a broader struggle for independence from colonial repression.

On 19 April 1960, the OPO was formally reconstituted as the **South West Africa People's Organisation (SWAPO).**[1] SWAPO's central objective was and is the liberation of the Namibian people from colonial oppression and exploitation in all its forms.

SWAPO

SWAPO has pursued its political aims of national liberation for Namibia through negotiations, mass organisation inside Namibia, international campaigning and armed struggle.

SWAPO's headquarters are in Luanda (Angola) and it maintains offices in a number of other countries.

At a national congress in Windhoek in 1961, SWAPO decided that political and military struggle in pursuit of national liberation were not contradictory but were complementary and should be pursued concurrently. The launching of armed struggle on 26 August 1966 became a part of SWAPO's strategy while the leadership continued to indicate its preparedness, under certain conditions, to negotiate and welcomed United Nations efforts to promote a peaceful settlement.

Years of intensive campaign work inside Namibia have gained SWAPO wide support, and the guerilla activities are rooted in the wider political work the movement has been engaged in. Informal study groups have been set up throughout the country to discuss the political situation; public education and mobilisation has been carried out by the SWAPO Youth League, its Elders' Council and Women's Council. Public meetings have taken place frequently and SWAPO guerilla fighters undergo political as well as military training.

Although SWAPO has never been formally banned by South Africa, massive arrests and repression have made open political activities increasingly difficult. SWAPO's office in Windhoek has been repeatedly raided by police and its workers detained for questioning.[2] Nevertheless, SWAPO supporters inside Namibia continue to organise political activities such as public rallies.

SWAPO's external wing is engaged in representing the movement internationally and in negotiations, raising support for the armed struggle and coordinating it. It operates extensive educational and relief programmes for Namibian refugees in Angolan and Zambian camps, setting up self-help schemes, schools and hospitals.

SWAPO'S NATIONAL SUPPORT

SWAPO's opponents often claim that its support comes mainly from the Ovambo tribe, and that it is not representative of the Namibian people as a whole. While clearly Ovambos are among SWAPO's most numerous supporters, they are also the largest group of the Namibian population (40–50%) and will, in any independent government, form a majority of voters and representatives. SWAPO's Executive Committee includes Namibians from a number of groups, and support comes from among the whole population.[3] The groups who joined SWAPO in 1976 for example represented people from central and southern Namibia.[4]

INTERNATIONAL SUPPORT FOR SWAPO

SWAPO has successfully secured support and recognition from international organisations and many countries. It was recognized as the liberation movement of the Namibian people by the Organisation of African Unity (OAU) in 1965. In 1973 the United Nations General Assembly accepted SWAPO as the authentic representative of the Namibian people, granting it full observer status at the General Assembly in 1976 (SWAPO is the only liberation movement to achieve this status), and participation rights in all UN agencies.[5]

SWAPO has received substantial material aid from a number of organisations. The OAU donated large amounts through its African Liberation Committee, and religious organisations such as the World Council of Churches and the Lutheran World Federation have given money for educational work and help with refugees. Many African countries provide bilateral aid to SWAPO, as well as giving sanctuary and educational facilities to Namibian refugees. Among European countries, Sweden has steadily increased its aid to SWAPO.[6]

SWAPO'S POLICIES

At a meeting in Lusaka in July/August 1976, SWAPO adopted a Constitution which outlines SWAPO's basic aims and objectives and the policies a SWAPO government would adopt in an independent Namibia.

The Constitution pledges that SWAPO will "fight relentlessly for immediate and total liberation of Namibia from colonialist and imperialist occupation", and will aim to unite all the people of Namibia, irrespective of race, religion, sex or ethnic origin into a cohesive, representative, national political entity.

It stresses opposition to racism, tribalism and sexism, and envisages the establishment in Namibia of a democratic, secular government founded upon the will and participation of all the Namibian people. Such a government would exercise effective control over the means of production and distribution and pursue a policy which facilitates the way to social ownership of all the resources of the country. Its stated aim is to work towards the creation of a non-exploitative and non-oppressive classless society.[7] The Political Programme adopted together with the Constitution lays down in more detail the areas of SWAPO's concern. Domestically, these include the need for agricultural development to achieve self-sufficiency, the creation of an integrated, national economy with a proper

45

balance between agricultural and industrial developments, and an emphasis on collective ownership. It stresses the need for education and training to enable Namibians to acquire needed skills, and to develop peoples' cultural creativeness. It aims at providing free and universal education for all Namibians, as well as a comprehensive, free medical service with emphasis on preventive medicine.

The Programme stresses the need for a deep-going transformation of the Namibian society which has so far been subjected to policies imposed by outside powers.

THE SOUTH WEST AFRICA
NATIONAL UNION (SWANU)

SWANU was founded in 1959 by Herero students and intellectuals. Its stated aim was to unite the people of South West Africa into one national front. In the early 1960's SWANU won a brief recognition from the Organisation of African Unity from 1963 to 1965. Attempts to unite with SWAPO failed partly because of the different tactics the movements pursued.

While SWAPO embarked on armed struggle and won wide international recognition, SWANU decided not to organise externally. It has remained essentially a small movement of intellectuals whose support comes largely from the Hereros.

Further short-lived attempts were made in the 1970's to form an alliance involving SWAPO, SWANU and a number of anti-colonial groups. SWANU is now the dominant member of the **Namibia National Front,** a centralist alliance, which transformed itself into a political party in April 1980. SWANU has frequently expressed anti-SWAPO opinions, rejecting the claim that SWAPO is the sole representative of the Namibian people (as recognised by the UN) and presenting itself, in the Namibia National Front, as a reasonable alternative.

SWANU has built up its support base through its radical rhetoric but has in reality done little to transform this rhetoric into practice. It opposes any solution to conflict which will effectively exclude it from the reigns of power, and sees the Namibia National Front as a vehicle to counter SWAPO's popularity.

SOLIDARITY AGAINST APARTHEID

A number of political groups in Namibia have shown their opposition to apartheid by joining into loose alliance at different times.

In 1972, SWAPO was instrumental in forming the **National Convention of Namibia** to unite all anti-colonialist groups in Namibia. SWAPO withdrew in 1975, having found that leading figures in the National Convention of Namibia such as Chief Clemens Kapuuo were openly collaborating with South Africa in the Turnhalle Constitutional Conference. The **Namibia National Convention** was formed the same year, drawing together SWAPO, SWANU and a number of other political groups, on a basis of total opposition to separate development and the Turnhalle Conference. Following disagreements, SWAPO withdrew in 1976 and most of the other groups formally disbanded themselves and joined SWAPO.

THE MIDDLE GROUND

A political alliance, the **Namibian National Front (NNF)** was formed in April 1977 by eight parties and tribal groups, including SWANU, three Damara groups, and others. The white **Federal Party** joined the Namibia National Front in March 1978 but resigned in June 1979. In its policy manifesto, the NNF sees itself as anti-racist and as trying to achieve national unity rather than ethnic identity. It presents itself as a moderate alternative to SWAPO and favours a pro-capitalist approach in an independent Namibia.

SWANU's domination of the NNF led to tensions with the other groups, and membership has fluctuated as groups have broken away, some to join SWAPO.

In May 1978, the NNF set up a working alliance with the **SWAPO-Democrats,** an organisation formed by former SWAPO member, Andreas Shipanga. Moves began in September 1979 to achieve a merger, between the NNF and SWAPO-Democrats and to restructure the umbrella organisation into a political party. However, the founding congress in April 1980 was marked by disagreements. SWAPO-Democrats did not attend, and two groups, the **National Independence Party** and the **Rehoboth Group,** walked out. The new party, which retains the name Namibia National Front, consists of SWANU, the **Progressive Party,** the **Damara Council** and the **Mbanderu Group** under Chief Munjuku. It continues to be heavily dominated by SWANU.[8]

SWAPO-DEMOCRATS

The formation of SWAPO-Democrats was announced in June 1978 in Sweden, by Andreas Shipanga, former SWAPO Information Secretary, and his supporters. The new party is strongly opposed to SWAPO. Shipanga has made a number of personal attacks on SWAPO's President, Sam Nujoma, and claims that SWAPO is intent on frustrating any election process inside Namibia and has no intention of operating in a peaceful way.[9]

Andreas Shipanga was among a number of senior SWAPO members to be arrested in Zambia in 1976, after having reportedly challenged Sam Nujoma's leadership. He was released, with 18 others, from detention in Tanzania, to where they had been moved, in May 1978, and returned to Namibia in August. There has been persistent speculation that SWAPO-Democrats may align itself with the Namibia National Front.

Mr. Shipanga claims that some 1,800 SWAPO members were arrested in Zambia in 1976 and are being held in detention on request from SWAPO's leader. This has been denied both by Mr. Nujoma and the Zambian government. The issue was publicised when negotiations took place about the exchange of prisoners in preparation for possible elections.[10] When challenged by the United Nations Commissioner for Namibia, Mr. Ahtisaari, to substantiate his claims with a list of names of the alleged detainees, SWAPO-Democrats claimed to have handed a list of 100 names to Mr. Ahtisaari in 1977. No full list has ever been produced by SWAPO-Democrats, however.[11]

SWAPO-Democrats have refused to participate in the National Assembly set up by South Africa, and are in favour of United Nations supervised elections. The party rejects armed struggle and sees itself as an alternative to SWAPO. The organisation experienced bitter internal strife in early 1980 and expelled two of its leading members, the Publicity and Information Secretary, Dr. K. Abrahams, and the Secretary General, Mrs. Otile Abrahams.[12]

The White Power Structure

THE PUBLIC SERVICE

Political control in Namibia is vested in a number of white-dominated bodies such as the Public Service and the Administrator General's office which have direct links with South Africa, and white or white-dominated parties which derive their legitimacy through varying degrees of accommodation with South Africa's plans for the future of Namibia.

The Public Service is staffed by 15,000 South Africans and is considered the controlling political force among whites. Its members have shown strong resistance to even moderate reforms in race relations, and are among the main supporters of the right wing South West Africa National Party's front organisation, Aktur (see below)[13]

The Public Service has undergone restructuring as South Africa attempts to create the impression that Namibia is moving towards "responsible self-government".

A number of government functions previously carried out by South African government departments have been transferred to ten "Directorates" established for that purpose.[14] They form the basis for establishing an ostensibly "independent" Namibian Public Service in terms of the *Government Service Bill* adopted by the National Assembly in May 1980, which provided for the directorates to become departments headed by secretaries in what was termed a "new" government service. In practice, South Africa retains control, through its appointed

Administrator General, who heads the Directorates. Key departments such as Security and Foreign Affairs continue to be directly controlled and administered by South Africa.

About 300 public servants had been recruited by September 1979.[15] Many South Africans employed in the administrative structures of Namibia are likely to retain control on the basis of secondment.

WHITE POLITICAL PARTIES

The **National Party** of South Africa has historically close links with its counterpart in South Africa, supporting the same policies of separate development for Namibia as in the Republic.

From 1950 to 1977, all Namibian representatives in the South African parliament were National Party members. Namibian representation in the South African Parliament was abolished in 1977.

The National Party strongly opposes changes in petty apartheid such as those enacted in the *Abolishment of Racial Discrimination (Urban Residential Areas and Public Amenities) Act* of July 1979, which makes provision for opening white residential areas and removing racial discrimination from restaurants, hotels etc. It lost a court case in which it challenged the power of the National Assembly to pass such legislation, and withdrew from the Assembly in protest.[16] At its annual congress in July 1979, it accused South Africa's Foreign Minister of "surrendering the whites of the territory."[17]

The **Herstigte National Party (HNP),** an extreme right wing party, was established in South Africa in 1969 after a split in the National Party. While it has little electoral support in Namibia, (it obtained 5,781 out of 326,264 votes in the 1978 internal elections), its stirring of white fears about the terrible consequences of a "sell-out" by South Africa to the United Nations has gained it increasing white sympathies. One top nationalist leader claimed that the National Party and Herstigte National Party have almost total backing from key security services, and that the police would not fire a shot at members of a white-led movement.[18]

The **Federal Party (FP)** grew out of the **United National Party of South West Africa** which was formed in 1927 and dissolved in 1975. During 1977, the Federal Party declared itself a non-racial political force and in favour of national reconciliation. This it reaffirmed in a statement of "Points of View and Priorities" which also re-emphasised the need for an internationally acceptable solution and urged direct discussions between the South African government, SWAPO and the Front Line States. It warned the authorities "not to ignore the lessons of Zimbabwe", and rejected participation in the National Assembly in its present form, and in white elections.[19]

The **Republican Party (RP)** was formed in 1977 by Dirk Mudge, a prominent member of the white delegation to the Turnhalle Constitutional Conference, after his challenge for the leadership of the National Party was defeated. At its annual congress in September 1979, the Republican Party declared its support for South Africa's security forces remaining in Namibia, and demanded independence as soon as possible, even without international recognition.[20]

WHITE ALLIANCES

In late 1977, two new political alliances, the **Democratic Turnhalle Alliance (DTA)** and the **Action Front for the Retention of the Turnhalle Principles (Aktur)** emerged. Both have their roots in the Turnhalle Constitutional Conference. The Democratic Turnhalle Alliance was formed by Dirk Mudge as an alliance between his Federal Party and the majority of the black groups who had taken part in the Conference. The National Party and a few black leaders joined to form Aktur. A major difference between the two parties is their interpretation of the Turnhalle Constitution (see Ch. XIII) and their plans for a future Namibia. The DTA, which dominates the South African-created National Assembly, wishes to see that body transformed into the effective executive and legislative authority for the territory, overriding all other government bodies. While declaring itself in favour of continued negotiations with the United Nations for an international settlement, it has increasingly pressed for independence at all costs.[21] The DTA takes a strongly anti-SWAPO platform. It receives considerable financial support from South Africa and the Federal Republic of Germany.[22] In October 1978, the **Interessengemeinschaft Deutschsprachiger Südwester (IG),** which represents prominent German-speaking residents in Namibia and has close links with right wing parties in the Federal Republic of Germany, donated ten vehicles equipped with 16 mm film projectors and screens to the DTA for its election campaign.[23] A prominent DTA member reportedly admitted that the DTA was receiving private funds from right wing German political sources.[24]

Aktur is determined to retain an ethnic structure of government for Namibia, based on the second tier authorities of the existing homeland "governments", and is strongly opposed to giving the National Assembly more power.

EXTREME RIGHT-WING GROUPINGS

Two white resistance movements, both pledging armed revolt against racial integration, were formed in February 1979. The **White Resistance Movement (WWB)** formed by a group of German speaking people, claimed to have compiled a death list and threatened to assassinate a number of prominent personalities. A hand grenade attack on the Masonic Lodge in Windhoek, in which one man was killed and 4 injured, is believed to have been the work of the WWB. The movement has carried on smear campaigns against Freemasons and

Jews, and distributed pamphlets listing "enemies of the White race."[25]

Another group, **Blank SWA** (South West Africa) was formed by a group of young Afrikaans-speaking men feeling frustrated with the National Party.[26] It is said to include members of both the NP and the HNP, as well as of the South African Afrikaner secret organisation, the Broederbond.[27]

XII   The War in Namibia

THE ARMED LIBERATION STRUGGLE

In accordance with a decision taken at its national congress in 1961 that political and military efforts should be pursued concurrently, SWAPO's military wing, the People's Liberation Army of Namibia (PLAN), has carried out increasingly successful guerilla operations, attacking South African military targets and holding down a large number of South African troops in Namibia.

The early years of the fighting, which began in 1966, presented considerable logistical problems of supply and communications for the guerillas. Fighting units had to operate from bases in neighbouring Zambia. All the inhabited parts of Namibia except Eastern Caprivi and Okavango were separated from these bases by hundreds of miles of dry country controlled by the Portuguese army in Angola. During the first nine years, fighting was of necessity restricted to northeastern Namibia, concentrating on ambushes of South African patrols and convoys, raids and mining of military roads. SWAPO units depended on and received support from the local population for concealment and supply of necessities.

From being a small force operating mainly in Eastern Caprivi and Okavango, the guerilla force grew and mounted increasingly successful operations throughout the north and infiltrated the centre and the south of the country.

Angolan independence in 1975 signalled a new phase in the liberation struggle, giving SWAPO bases in Angola from which to expand its guerilla activities and to open new military zones inside Namibia. In 1975, SWAPO reportedly had 1,000 guerillas, and had established several bases in southern Angola close to the Caprivi Strip.[1]

1976 saw a sharp increase in guerilla activities, with scores of reported attacks by PLAN and skirmishes with the South African Defence Force. PLAN inflicted considerable damage on the white occupation machinery and on strategic installations. For example, in 1977, SWAPO guerillas damaged buildings at the Ruacana power station, destroyed a water tower in Ovamboland, partially derailed a train and destroyed a major water supply line. In February 1978, telephone poles and pylons were blown up in central and western Ovamboland, a bridge sabotaged, and the South African military base at Elundu, 10 km south of the Angolan border, bombarded. In April and May that year, guerillas attacked two other South African military bases.[2]

In April 1979, members of PLAN blew up a power supply line near the Ruacana hydro-electric power plant on the Kunene River, and a week earlier they bombarded the town of Ruacana which houses hundreds of South African soldiers.[3]

The South African Prime Minister admitted in May 1979 that there had been an increase in guerilla activities in Namibia since the beginning of the year, and that patrols by the South African Police and Defence Force were being intensified.[4]

SWAPO's policy of gaining support among the local population has enabled it to establish areas in the north where South African troops are reluctant to go. A Swedish film team, which visited these areas in 1978, reported that SWAPO personnel were providing medical care and transport and produced food, encouraging the people to be self-sufficient.[5]

SWAPO officials point out that the military activities of PLAN now cover the entire country and are not confined to the border area. The strategy is not only to engage South African troops in combat but to launch attacks on carefully selected economic targets in order to destroy the infrastructure which ensures the supply lines of the enemy.[6]

In February 1980, the South African military commander in Namibia, General Geldenhuys, admitted that since the beginning of 1980, SWAPO had escalated its activities, strike groups were appearing in greater numbers, and infiltration from Angola had increased.[7]

In April 1980, Namibia was virtually blacked out twice within two weeks as PLAN again sabotaged the power lines at the Ruacana hydro-electric station.[8] Other attacks were made on railway lines and telephone poles.

SOUTH AFRICAN MILITARY BUILD-UP

South Africa's military presence in Namibia amounts to an army of occupation. By 1979 more than 60,000 troops were engaged in fighting SWAPO guerillas, patrolling the northern areas and policing the local population.[9]

The military build-up has coincided with periods of heightened protest inside Namibia, of increases in military activities by SWAPO, and of deepening political entrenchment by South Africa such as the December 1978 elections and the creation of the National Assembly in May 1979.

Until 1972, security operations were carried out by armed South African police. During the general strike of 1971/2, South African troops were sent into the territory, breaking up strike meetings and carrying out large scale arrests.[10]

South African troops used Namibia as a springboard for the invasion of Angola in 1975, and established a number of new major bases in the territory. A large military camp, with a base for the South African Defence Forces's Logistic Supply Command, was set up at Grootfontein. By 1977, South Africa had established some 20 military bases throughout Namibia.[11] After the forced withdrawal from Angola in March 1976, the South African troops remained stationed in Namibia. The UN Commissioner for Namibia estimated in 1976 that South Africa had a total of 45,000 troops in Namibia, including 1,900 police counter insurgency units and 26,300 logistics support forces.[12] In addition, the South African Air Force maintains a major base at Rooikop in Walvis Bay which has all the necessary facilities to serve an air strike force. The harbour of Walvis Bay is guarded by South African marines who use sophisticated radar equipment and armed harbour patrol boats.[13] Two of the South African army's elite units are stationed in the area.

As South Africa prepared for internal elections in Namibia in late 1978, a vast increase in air and ground forces was reported. A small airfield was enlarged to take French Mirage bombers, military roads were extended and more patrols and road blocks set up.[14]

A new and more intense phase of the war began in 1979 with a military build-up which coincided with the creation of the National Assembly in May 1979. One journalist commented that "South Africa has mobilised thousands of military reservists to reinforce army units in northern Namibia, where one of the biggest operations in the 13 year war against nationalist guerillas is said to be underway. Hundreds of trucks, troop carriers and armoured vehicles have been moved north through Windhoek in convoys often several miles long".[15]

In June, reports spoke of an unprecedented psychological and military campaign being carried out against SWAPO in northern Namibia. Road blockades, military barricades and protection posts were set up on the main road to the Angolan frontier. Continuous movement of armoured cars with 16 mm cannons mounted on them was observed. Dozens of Africans from villages in the region were arrested.[16] During one month, from 16 April to 16 May 1979, South Africa reported 68 separate incidents involving SWAPO fighters and South African forces.[17]

The militarisation of Namibia has continued to increase and intensify. One SWAPO leader spoke of "daily eyewitness reports of trainloads of South African soldiers arriving in Namibia with a view to reinforce the occupationist army". He estimated the number of South African troops in April 1980 at well over 80,000.[18]

In late 1979, the South African army was reportedly planning to buy about 60,000 hectares of land east of Okahandja, occupying vacated farms and purchasing others, to transform them into military bases for training and development of troops and equipment.[19] In March 1980, the mayor of Okahandja reported that 2,167 hectares of land had been sold to the South African Defence Force (SADF) for R43,350,000, and that a training college was to be erected by the army in the town.[20]

SOUTH AFRICA'S STRATEGY OF TOTAL WAR

South Africa's military presence in Namibia pervades the entire life of the local population. The General Secretary of Lutheran World Ministries, who visited Namibia in 1979, stressed that "evidence of South African army brutality among all segments of the population is overwhelming, pervasive and capable of documentation". In Ovamboland, the people are "totally at the mercy of the arbitrary power of the South African army and of the Home Guard, comprised of young, black dropouts from Ovambo society . . . These armed bands, often undisciplined, are known for committing atrocities against their own people."[21]

Since the 1970's, South Africa has mounted a civil action programme aimed at "winning the hearts and minds of the people." Recognising that SWAPO's success is rooted in support from the local population, South African military experts assert that 80% of the war has to be fought at the psychological level. South African troops have taken on tasks as teachers, agricultural advisors and doctors. Suspicion from the local population has made this a limited success, and the repressive role of the security forces have been continually evident. In addition to the Permanent Force and the National Servicemen, who are called up for 24 months, between 8,000 and 10,000 Citizen Force reservists have been mobilised in South Africa for deployment in Namibia.[22]

In 1977, a SWA Specialist Unit of handpicked national servicemen and Permanent Force members was created consisting of expert trackers on foot who use dogs, a mounted section and a motorcycle unit.[23] They are backed up by Commando units from the local white population who are trained by South African military experts. The South African police perform essentially military functions, having powers to search, question and detain people under special security regulations which were extended over 50% of the country on 10 May 1979 and amount to virtual martial law.

THE CREATION OF THE
SOUTH WEST AFRICA DEFENCE FORCE

Plans for a Namibian national army, trained, selected and controlled by South Africa and ready to take over as a cover for South Africa's continued presence in Namibia took shape with the public introduction of a South West Africa Defence Force (SWADF) in September 1979. In May 1980 it was announced that the Windhoek administration would be given control over it.[24] The Administrator General made it clear, however, that even after the transfer of indigenous units of the security forces to the Namibian authorities, the South African Defence Force and Police would continue to play a major role in Namibia, and South Africa would retain control over the overall security situation.

One of the main reasons for transferring South West Africa units of the defence forces to the Windhoek administration, he said, was that national service for all "population groups" would most likely be introduced by 1981.[25]

This fits in with plans announced by the South African military command in Namibia to reduce the number of South African troops engaged in border duty by as much as 50% and replace them with local black and white personnel. A 40% increase in the number of Namibians doing operational duty during 1980 was envisaged.[26] By mid-1979, troops from the South West Africa Command already made up an estimated one third of the forces in the "operational area".[27]

South Africa has been training ethnically segregated tribal armies in Namibia for a number years, starting with a Bushman unit in western Caprivi in 1974. The new South African military commander appointed to Namibia in August 1977

55

was given the task of building up a multi-racial defence force. 41 Batallion, consisting of recruits from a number of "ethnic groups", was created to form the skeleton of the future SWADF, though separate tribally-based armies continue to exist.[28]

In August 1980, all Namibian units were transferred from the SADF into the newly named SWA Territory Force, nominally under the control of the "Council of Ministers" established in July 1980 (*see Ch. XIII, Executive and legislative organs*). In practice, the SADF remains directlu responsible for overall security in the territory.

ATTACKS ON NEIGHBOURING COUNTRIES

South Africa uses Namibia as a base for attacks into neighbouring Zambia and Angola. Since South Africa's humiliating defeat in Angola in early 1976, the South African airforce has flown regular reconnaissance flights into southern Angola, and South African troops have attacked Angolan villages, killed civilians and destroyed their homes on the pretext of "hot pursuit" of SWAPO units.[29]

The most brutal attack which aroused international horror took place just before SWAPO was due to sign an agreed procedure for independence elections with the Western powers in May 1978. On 4 May, South African troops launched a major military attack into Angola, destroying a Namibian refugee camp and attacking the nearby town of Kassinga. While 300-700 ground troops crossed to attack some small SWAPO camps in southern Angola, South African planes bombed Kassinga 150 miles north from 6 a.m. to 6 p.m. dropping paratroopers and reinforcements. The camp housed 4,000 to 5,000 refugees, many recent arrivals. Casualty figures given by the Angolan authorities amounted to 600 dead and 1,000 wounded, including many children. South Africa claimed that Kassinga was a major military base of PLAN, but accounts from representatives of international organisations clearly showed it to be a refugee camp.[30]

In July 1979, the Angolan government submitted a comprehensive report to the UN Secretary-General on the *Human casualties and material and other damage resulting from repeated acts of aggression by the racist regime of South Africa against the People's Republic of Angola*.[31] The report recorded in detail each act of South African aggression against Angola from March 1976 to June 1979.

During this period, the SADF were responsible for 94 air space violations, 21 ground infiltrations, 21 border provocations, 7 artillery bombardments, 193 armed mine-laying operations, 25 attacks by ground forces, 24 aerial attacks and one large combined operation of ground and air forces. As a result, at least 1,383 people were killed and 1,800 wounded. The report stated that the attacks "resulted in the destruction of the country's basic infrastructures". They were "aimed at creating a climate of insecurity and fear, and are part of a concerted plan for the destabilisation of political, social and economic life in the People's Republic of Angola in particular and in southern Africa as a whole".

In a letter made public in September 1979, the Zambian representative at the UN stated that between January and September 1979, South African warplanes, ground and waterborne troops violated Zambian land and air space, carrying out "indiscriminate acts" of aggression against innocent inhabitants. The letter stated that these attacks had increased in frequency and intensity, thereby threatening the security and peace of the region.[32]

These attacks have intensified as South Africa has reformulated its strategy in the wake of election victory by the liberation movements in Zimbabwe. They aim to force the Front Line States into lessening their support for SWAPO, and thus isolate the liberation movement.

Zambia reported attacks by South African military aircraft and troops on villages in its Western Province in February 1980, and called an urgent meeting of the UN Security Council on 10 April which condemned South Africa's aggression and passed a resolution demanding the immediate withdrawal of all South African troops from Zambian territory. Angola reported in February 1980 that several thousand South African soldiers were massing on its border with Namibia in preparation for an airborne assault. On 7 June 1980, South African forces launched a major attack on Angola, occupying large parts of two southern Angolan provinces and causing hundreds of human casualties. While South Africa claimed that it had aimed to destroy SWAPO bases in Angola, the Angolan government said that the invasion, involving the largest number of South African troops in any attack since 1975-6, was aimed at capturing key points inside the proposed demilitarized zone and installing members of UNITA (see Chapter XIII, Alternative Strategies). The South African operation, which continued for a month, was condemned by the UN Security Council, though Britain, France and the United States abstained. The Council adopted a resolution strongly condemning the racist regime of South Africa for its premeditated, persistent and sustained armed invasions of Angola, and South Africa's utilization of the international territory of Namibia "as a springboard for armed invasions and destabilization" of Angola. The resolution also called upon all states to implement fully the arms embargo imposed against South Africa by the Council in November 1977.[33] South Africa has consistently backed bands of UNITA soldiers, a former Angolan nationalist movement which collaborated with the South African invasion of Angola of 1975-6, in their harassment of villages in southern Angola. A large number of UNITA supporters are reportedly in camps in northern Namibia and are being trained by the South African Defence Force.[34]

South Africa's aggression against neighbouring countries clearly represents a threat to peace not only in the region, but at an international level. As South Africa becomes more isolated, it makes more desperate attempts at arresting history.

REFUGEES

Thousands of Namibians have been forced to flee into exile to escape from the war and widespread repression which is particularly severe in the northern part of the country. Many young people have left to join SWAPO's external wing for military training.

Between June 1974 and early 1975, over 6,000 people crossed the border into southern Angola and made their way to Zambia. They were fleeing from the floggings, arrests and harassment that were affecting their daily lives.[35]

From June 1978, when the South African government began registering voters for its own version of general elections, refugees were crossing the border at rates of up to 500 a week. There are now over 40,000 Namibians in exile.[36]

Many refugees live under SWAPO's care in Zambia and Angola. At Nyango, six hours drive from Lusaka, a settlement and a school for between 2,500 and 3,000 adults and children has been built in the bush.[37]

Since the liberation of Angola in 1975, refugee camps have been set up there. The majority of Namibian exiles now live in these camps. They are exposed to frequent harassment from the SADF who bomb the camps on the pretext that they are SWAPO bases. SWAPO, the United Nations High Commission for Refugees and the Angolan government cooperate in supplying the settlements with their basic needs. SWAPO has encouraged self-help schemes in education and health and the people in the camps themselves build their own clinics and schools.

In Lusaka, Zambia, the United Nations Institute for Namibia gives some of the refugees a chance to study.

XIII Alternative Strategies for an Independent Namibia

EXTERNAL AND INTERNAL PRESSURES

South Africa has engaged in a number of manoeuvres to maintain control over Namibia, defying international opinion as expressed in United Nations resolutions and by the International Court of Justice (*see Ch. III, South Africa and the UN*).

Negotiations for an internationally recognised settlement involving the UN, SWAPO, South Africa and, from April 1977, the "Contact Group" consisting of the then five Western members of the UN Security Council (United States, Britain, France, Federal Republic of Germany, Canada) have continued at a slow pace governed by South African delaying tactics and Western unwillingness to apply effective pressure. Meanwhile, South Africa has implemented changes in Namibia which are taking the territory rapidly towards an unofficial unilateral declaration of independence.

In the early 1970s, South Africa came under a variety of pressures, which led it to find means of pursuing its policies in Namibia while appearing to yield to international opinion. After two years' effort, the UN discontinued its policy of "dialogue" with the South African government in December 1973. The April 1974 coup in Portugal and the subsequent emergence of an independent government in Angola in 1975 facilitated SWAPO guerilla operations inside Namibia. South Africa suffered a humiliating political and military defeat when its invading forces were driven out of Angola in early 1976 by the forces of the Angolan liberation movement MPLA with assistance from Cuba.

The idea of a constitutional conference in Namibia, ostensibly to debate freely the future of the territory, was presented by Pretoria in an attempt to sidestep these pressures.

THE TURNHALLE CONSTITUTIONAL CONFERENCE

In September 1974, the leader of the SWA National Party announced a plan to hold constitutional talks about the future of Namibia, and a Constitutional Conference opened at the Turnhalle in Windhoek in September 1975. It was attended by representatives from 11 "population groups" and a white delegation—a strategy which continued the division of Namibia along racial and tribal lines. While South Africa claimed that the Conference could debate all options for independence, only those leaders who accepted the initial division and were prepared to represent specific "population groups" were eligible to attend. This automatically excluded SWAPO and others who rejected political organisation on a racial and tribal basis.

Within some of the homelands, opposition from political groups to the Turnhalle led to the hasty promotion of new, more compliant "leaders", and allegations of South African interference in the selection of Turnhalle delegates were made for instance by Damara and Nama political groups. The Conference itself was marked by slow progress, avoidance of controversial issues, internal wrangles and the growing disenchantment of some groups with the whole exercise. A number of delegates demanded that political parties be invited to participate.[1]

SWAPO and the NNC (*see Ch. XI, Political Groupings*) repeatedly affirmed their total rejection of the Turnhalle talks, condemning them as a public relations exercise aimed at the perpetuation of white minority rule. SWAPO set out conditions under which it would be prepared to negotiate with South Africa, including the withdrawal of the South African police and army from Namibia, the lifting of emergency regulations, and acceptance by South Africa of national sovereignty for Namibia. During the Turnhalle proceedings, hundreds of SWAPO members and supporters were arrested and detained without trial.

In August 1976, the Constitutional Committee of the Turnhalle agreed on establishing an interim government and on achieving independence by December 1978. These proposals were rejected by the UN, the countries of the European Community and SWAPO. By the beginning of 1977 a draft constitution was completed, which provided for 11 ethnic governments, each separately elected by a particular ethnic group. A 60-member National Assembly would be formed from appointed delegates of each ethnic group. It would have strictly limited powers and could only reach decisions by consensus. In other words, the basis was laid for a compliant government which, while formally independent, would actually be controlled by South Africa.

INTERNATIONAL PRESSURES FOR A SETTLEMENT

Pressure on South Africa to abandon the plan for an ethnically divided government based on the Turnhalle proposals grew throughout the Conference period. SWAPO's military and diplomatic success, backed by strong support from African and other Third World states at the UN, played a significant part.

Following Angolan independence, the armed struggle escalated, stretching South African resources and gaining increasing support for SWAPO inside the country. In January 1976, the UN Security Council unanimously adopted Resolution 385 condemning South Africa's illegal occupation of Namibia, the brutal oppression of its people and the aggressive military build-up in the area, and demanding free elections under UN supervision.[2] However, the United States, Britain, France and West Germany repeatedly vetoed demands by the African states for the imposition of full economic sanctions against South Africa.[3] An arms embargo and a curb on all new loans and investments in the Republic were suggested in draft resolutions discussed by the African states in March 1977. In order to avoid another embarrassing veto, the "Contact Group" offered to help negotiate terms for the independence of Namibia, on the basis of free territory-wide elections under the aegis of the UN.

THE WESTERN INITIATIVE

The Western "Contact Group" held four rounds of talks during 1977, separately meeting the South African government, the Turnhalle representatives and SWAPO. Although the precise content of the discussions was kept secret, they were widely reported to have yielded certain compromises.

The Turnhalle Conference would be disbanded. South Africa would hold elections on the basis of universal adult suffrage with the participation of all political parties including SWAPO. An Administrator General (AG) would be installed in Namibia until independence. UN supervision and control would be established through a Special Representative appointed by the UN Secretary General. The Special Representative's central task would be to make sure that conditions were established allowing free and fair elections and an impartial electoral process. The AG would repeal discriminatory and repressive legislation. Disputes over the status of political prisoners would be resolved by a four-man commission. Law and order would remain the responsibility of South Africa. Throughout the negotiations, South Africa was opposed to withdrawing her troops from the territory prior to the elections.

On 1 September 1977, the South African-appointed Administrator General Justice M. T. Steyn took office in Windhoek. The previous office of Administrator was abolished. The provision made in the *South West Africa Affairs Amendment Act* No. 23 of 1949 for white voters of South West Africa to be represented by six members in the South African House of Assembly was abolished on 28 September 1977. In a pre-emptive move, South Africa issued a Proclamation on 31 August 1977 providing for Walvis Bay, which is an integral part of Namibia and had been administered as such since 1922, to be administered as part of the Cape Province of the Republic of South Africa, and to form part of the Cape electoral division of Namaqualand. None of the provisions negotiated with the Contact Group would therefore apply to Walvis Bay.[4]

After further extensive negotiations, the Western countries put forward a "Proposal for a Settlement in Namibia" on 30 March 1978. It contained the main factors agreed in the negotiations. An annex described provisions for the cessation of all hostile acts, and the restriction of South African and SWAPO armed forces to base. Thereafter, phased withdrawal from Namibia of all but 1,500 South African troops would take place within 12 weeks and prior to the start of the election campaign. The remaining South African troops would be restricted to one or two bases and would be withdrawn after certification of the elections. A United Nations Transition Assistance Group (Untag), with a military and civilian

61

component, would ensure that the provisions would be observed by all parties (*see Appendix*).

On 30 August 1978, at the request of the UN Security Council,[5] a Report by the UN Secretary General, Dr. Waldheim, on the implementation of the Western plan was published (*see Appendix*). On 29 September, the UN Security Council passed Resolution 435 endorsing the Waldheim Report (6). South Africa was faced with having to abandon its policy of separate, ethnically based elections and prove its commitment to hold free elections under UN supervision.

SOUTH AFRICA'S VOLTE FACE

Since the adoption of Resolution 435, all South Africa's efforts have been directed towards avoiding its implementation. In this, it has been effectively aided by the Western Contact Group's connivance in its delaying tactics. South Africa's real intentions for Namibia have been demonstrated in the continued promotion of apartheid policies while ostensibly agreeing to abandon the Turnhalle exercise in favour of a compromise with the UN.

Parallel with the negotiations with the Contact Group, South Africa continued to strengthen the homeland structure in Namibia (*see Ch. IV, The Bantustan governments*). The Turnhalle conference continued to meet at government expense until early 1978, and the South African Defence Force stepped up its programme to train tribal armies in Namibia. On 26 June 1978, the Administrator General began the registration of voters. This should have taken place only after a UN presence was established. Throughout the negotiations, South Africa had shown reluctance to relinquish military control. It had replaced earlier emergency regulations with new security measures which, while sounding more moderate, still allowed for wide measures of arrest, detention and control of movement. While some petty apartheid legislation had been repealed, racial oppression continued in practice. (*see Ch. V and VIII*).

South Africa seized the opportunity of the publication of the UN Report on the implementation of the Western Plan for Namibia to raise new objections. In a letter on 6 September 1978, the South African Foreign Minister centred his objections on the size of the proposed UN military force of 7,500, the executive powers of the UN police and date for elections.[7] He reported that South Africa was prepared to adhere to the Western proposals but not to "interpretations inconsistent with the proposals."[8]

SWAPO accepted the Waldheim Report in general. Despite UN and Western efforts to accommodate South African criticism, the South African government announced on 28 September 1978, the day when Mr. Vorster resigned as Prime Minister, that it would unilaterally hold elections in Namibia by December 1978, without UN supervision. The West failed to block this move. Efforts to salvage the Western Plan only met with assurances from the South African government that the elections would not lead to independence and should be regarded as an internal matter. South Africa would retain authority and claimed to be still willing to cooperate in the implementation of the Western Plan.

The UN Security Council and General Assembly passed resolutions condemning the internal elections, declaring them and their result null and void and stating that no recognition would be accorded either by the UN or any member state "to any representatives or organ established by that process.[9]

The failure of the Western initiative did not, however, produce any determination in the Contact Group to impose sanctions on South Africa as pressed by African leaders. Western and UN attempts to hold UN-supervised elections have continued to be met with further South African delaying tactics over the interpretation of the original Western Plan, and with new demands. There has been increasing contact between governments of the Contact Group and representatives of the "internal leadership" established as a result of the South African sponsored elections, contrary to the UN resolutions.

INTERNAL ELECTIONS

The unilateral elections held by South Africa in the territory on 4-8 December 1978 were preceded by widespread intimidation perpetrated by the South African Defence Force, white employers and the DTA to force people to register and take out DTA membership cards. This was documented in a number of reports.

A comprehensive document produced by the Christian Centre[10] in Windhoek found that people were beaten or threatened with loss of their jobs or refusal of medical treatment to force them to register. In some cases, voting took place in mobile polling booths manned by armed South African soldiers. The number of South African troops had been increased for the elections and their partisan influence was pervasive. Army vehicles carried DTA stickers. The entire government transport fleet was placed at the disposal of the DTA. There was a disturbing lack of secrecy at polling stations. The author of the Christian Centre report was deported from Namibia as a result of his observations.

The elections were condemned by SWAPO, which suffered widespread arrest and detention of its members during the period, by churches and the international community. A number of Namibian political groups, including SWANU and SWAPO, refused to participate.

The regime claimed a poll of over 80%, which must be measured against the background of intimidation on a massive scale. The election results gave the DTA a large majority of 41 seats in the newly created Constituent Assembly. The National Party gained 6 seats and 3 seats went to 3 smaller parties.[11]

CONSTITUTIONAL DEVELOPMENTS

The Constituent Assembly formed after the December 1978 internal elections was transformed into a National Assembly in May 1979. It was given limited powers and was described by the Judge President in Namibia as an "empty shell", unable to pass laws without ratification by the Administrator General, himself an appointee of the South African government.[12] The National Assembly has formed the basis for new constitutional arrangements leading to what South Africa describes as "responsible self-government". They are intended to give a semblance of power to internal structures established by South Africa and to increase pressure on the United Nations to include representatives of the internal "government" in international negotiations.

On 1 July 1980, a number of constitutional changes were promulgated by the Administrator General, creating a pyramid structure of institutions. At the top of the pyramid is the South African government which retains full control over foreign affairs, overall planning and command over the defence of the territory, and full authority with regard to international negotiations. Inside Namibia, the Administrator General carries out South Africa's policies. Local institutions have been established which retain the racial and ethnic divisions which have formed an essential basis for all South African policies in Namibia. An "independent" civil service has been created, and a Government Service Commission set up. In practice, South African public servants "seconded" to Namibia continue to occupy top positions and have been assured that they will not be affected by the new dispensation.[13]

EXECUTIVE AND LEGISLATIVE ORGANS

On 1 July 1980, a 12-man Council of Ministers replaced the previous Administrator General's Advisory Council. This had been set up in July 1979 with purely advisory functions and consisted of 12 DTA members.

The Council of Ministers, the equivalent of a "cabinet", is the executive organ of the new "government". Its chairman, Dirk Mudge, the leader of the DTA, was elected by the National Assembly which then elected the other eleven members on the proposal of the chairman. They are the same DTA members, representing the 11 "population groups", who previously sat on the Administrator General's Advisory Council.

The powers of the Council of Ministers are strictly circumscribed by the AG's authority to veto any decisions it takes. Some 20 government departments, previously called "directorates", come under its authority, including the new Department of Defence established in August 1980 which controls the SWA Territory Force (the former SWA Defence Force). Ministers are not responsible for specific departments but make collective decisions. The National Assembly has been given powers to draft legislation. The Council of Ministers makes decisions regarding the administration of laws. Its "directions, directives or policy" are carried out—with important reservations—by the AG. As head of the Executive Authority, the AG retains overall power over the Minister's Council, and, through his authority to make laws by Proclamation on certain matters and veto legislation drafted by the National Assembly, over that body. He can refer any matter back to each body with recommendations for reconsideration. In fact, the AG is "empowered to intervene at any moment in the legislative and executive process within the territory".[15]

BANTUSTANS WITH A NEW NAME

The constitutional changes implemented in the territory on 1 July 1980 have entrenched South Africa's policy of dividing Namibia along racial and ethnic lines. A three tier system has been established in which the National Assembly and Council of Ministers form the first tier central government, and the "homelands" are at second tier level. The third tier consists of municipal and village boards. Behind the new names are in fact the same tribally-based, South African-selected bodies which were first established under the Odendaal Plan and which later sent representatives to the Turnhalle Conference.

Each second tier authority has received a new constitution, formalising these cosmetic changes. The homeland "governments" no longer have "cabinet ministers" and a "chief minister" but a legislative assembly and an executive committee. Elections for representative authorities have been announced for each "population group," to take place in the autumn of 1980. Bodies such as the Coloured Council and the Nama Representative Council who had not been given "governments" previously, have been converted into legislative and executive institutions. A white representative authority has also been established, and a number of functions previously carried out by the white Legislative Assembly have been transferred to the central government. The ethnic, second tier authorities have been given jurisdiction over certain limited functions pertaining to their "population group". These include matters relating to land tenure, agriculture, education up to standard 10, health, social welfare and pensions, housing, art and culture, income tax and personal tax etc. Though it was stressed that no "population group" would be forced to establish second tier authorities, in practice new "ethnic representatives" loyal to South Africa's bantustan policy were being appointed by the AG to ensure compliance.

Immediately after the installation of these structures, Dirk Mudge the "chairman" of the Minister's Council, who has been referred to as "Prime Minister", went on a promotion tour to Western Europe where he was received by members of the German, French and British governments.[16]

INTERNATIONAL NEGOTIATIONS IN 1979 AND 1980

Throughout 1979, efforts to achieve an agreement for the implementation of Security Council Resolution 435 (1978), the UN Plan for elections in Namibia, were stalled by South Africa's objections to certain provisions in the UN Plan. These centred specifically on SWAPO bases inside Namibia and the supervision of SWAPO bases in neighbouring countries.

A proposal by the late President Neto of Angola to establish a 50 km wide demilitarised zone (DMZ) on both sides of Namibia's borders broke the deadlock temporarily. However, the plan for a DMZ evolved by representatives of the Contact Group and South Africa, without consultation with SWAPO, has little resemblance to the original idea. It provides for South Africa to retain "selected locations" in the DMZ, each consisting of a military base, its supporting airfield, population centre and the "immediate environment" of a radius of 5 kilometres from the perimeter of the installation or population centre. The plan also proposes that South African police would accompany the UN troops in the DMZ. SWAPO would not be allowed any bases in the DMZ.

Consultations took place in Geneva in November 1979 under the auspices of the UN on all aspects of the DMZ proposals drawn up by the Western Contact Group. On South Africa's insistence, a number of "internal parties" from Namibia also attended the talks. While both SWAPO and South Africa subsequently accepted the concept of a DMZ, interpretations differed widely. South Africa stipulated that agreement must be reached on a number of points, including the number of South African bases remaining in the DMZ, acceptable arrangements regarding the disarmament of SWAPO personnel, and confirmation that SWAPO would have no bases inside Namibia.[17] SWAPO strongly opposed the idea of disarming its guerillas, or removing them to a neighbouring country, pointing out that this would give undue advantage to the South African occupying army whose presence in Namibia is illegal.[18]

In February 1980, the newly appointed Untag Commander, General Prem Chand, visited Namibia, South Africa and the Front Line States to consult on the DMZ proposals. He was joined in Cape Town by the UN Special Representative for Namibia and a number of other officials for talks with the South African government, and met SWAPO officials in Angola. The UN Secretary General subsequently published a report on the visit which was handed to South Africa for consideration. It suggested a target date of 15 June 1980 for the implementation of the UN Plan.[19]

In its reply to the UN on 12 May 1980, South Africa set out further conditions disguised as questions for "clarification", clearly aimed at gaining time and at isolating SWAPO. They included a demand for 20 military bases inside the DMZ. This was offered as a "concession" from a previous demand for 40 bases. South Africa requested assurances that SWAPO would have no bases inside Namibia, that SWAPO personnel would be disarmed, and that the majority of Untag personnel would be deployed in the DMZ. South Africa also demanded that the UN accord equal recognition to the "internal parties" in Namibia in the international negotiations, withdraw recognition of SWAPO as the sole and authentic representative of the Namibian people, and cease all financial assistance to SWAPO. In addition, it stressed the need for UNITA, a former Angolan nationalist movement which over time has come to cooperate closely with the South African army, to be consulted. Western diplomats' reaction to these demands was that the South African response was "more constructive than expected".[20]

SWAPO's firm intention to speed up the implementation of Resolution 435 was shown in the further substantial concessions made to South Africa. Contrary to speculation that the DMZ proposal was dead, Dr. Waldheim's reply stated that SWAPO and the Front Line States agreed to 20 South African bases in the DMZ. The letter assured South Africa that upon South Africa's acceptance of the DMZ, and upon the implementation of Res. 435 (1978), the question of SWAPO bases in Namibia would no longer arise, and that Angola and Zambia had given assurances that there would be no infiltration of SWAPO personnel into Namibia. Five of Untag's seven battalions would be stationed in the DMZ. However, the UN would only deal with the parties envisaged in the Western settlement Plan, but would observe complete impartiality in the implementation of the Plan.[21] Western diplomats considered that Dr. Waldheim's reply had gone a long way towards satisfying South Africa's demands. If South Africa were not prepared to accept the assurances contained in the letter, "one must assume they are either trying to buy more time or else are not serious about going ahead with Resolution 435", one diplomat was reported as saying.[22]

South Africa's intensified attacks on Angola together with the moves towards "UDI" inside Namibia combine to confirm this view. Yet the West has continually avoided the issue of sanctions and has thus allowed South Africa to maintain and entrench its illegal occupation of Namibia.

Appendix I

CHRONOLOGY OF EVENTS

The following gives the main events in the international dispute over Namibia, and some significant dates in the history of Namibia itself.

1886/1890	Boundaries of German South West Africa determined in broad outline by agreements with Portugal and Britain.
1903–1907	Herero and Nama uprisings.
1915	South Africa invades and occupies South West Africa.
1919	In terms of Article 22 of the Covenant of the League of Nations, the SWA Mandate is conferred on Britain, to be exercised on its behalf by South Africa.
7 December 1920	SWA officially given as a 'C' Mandate to SA.
January 1946	SA, at the first UN General Assembly session, announces plans to consult population of SWA on proposed incorporation of the territory in the Union.
December 1946	UN General Assembly rejects SA proposal for incorporation. Invites SA to conclude trusteeship agreement. Rejected by SA.
May 1948	National Party gains power in SA.
July 1949	SA ceases to send reports to the UN.
December 1949	UN General Assembly requests ICJ to define the status of SWA.
July 1950	Court's Status Opinion rules that although South Africa is under no obligation to conclude a trusteeship agreement, the League of Nations Mandate continues in force with supervision to be exercised by the UN General Assembly.
April 1959	The Ovamboland People's Organisation launched in Windhoek.
November 1960	Ethiopia and Liberia initiate proceedings against South Africa before ICJ. General Assembly endorses move.
December 1960	The Ovamboland People's Organisation becomes the SWAPO.

1964	The Odendaal Report on the implementation of a bantustan programme submitted to the South Africa government.
July 1966	ICJ in SWA Judgement declares that Ethiopia and Liberia lack standing to obtain a judgement on the merits of the case.
August 1966	SWAPO launches armed struggle.
27 October 1966	General Assembly adopts resolution 2145 (XXI) revoking South Africa's Mandate over South West Africa. (114 yes, 2 no—Portugal and South Africa, 3 abstentions—France, Malawi, Britain).
May 1967	UN Council for Namibia created to administer the territory.
April 1968	South West Africa renamed Namibia by General Assembly resolution.
20 May 1969	UN Security Council declares South Africa's presence in Namibia illegal (Resolution 264, 13 yes, 2 abstentions —France, Britain).
July 1970	UN Security Council requests ICJ advisory opinion on legal consequences for status of South Africa's continued presence in Namibia.
June 1971	The ICJ rules that SA's continued presence in Namibia is illegal and SA is under obligation to withdraw its administration from the territory immediately. SA rejects opinion.
October 1971	The UN Security Council adopts Resolution 301 accepting the opinion of the ICJ.
March 1972	UN Secretary-General visits South Africa and Namibia and holds discussions with SA government officers in Pretoria.
8 October– 12 November, 1972	Dr. Alfred Esscher, as the UN Secretary-General's representative, visits Namibia and confers with the SA authorities in Pretoria.
11 December 1973	UN dialogue with SA is discontinued by unanimous decision by UN Security Council Resolution 342 (1973).
13 December 1973	The UN General Assembly recognises SWAPO "as the authentic representative of the Namibian people".
18 December 1973	Appointment of Mr. Sean McBride as UN Commissioner for Namibia.
16 May 1974	WHO admits Namibia as an associate member
22 April 1975	Ambassadors of the US, UK and France meet the SA Foreign Minister in Cape Town on the question of Namibia.

14 September 1975	Declaration of Intent by the Constitutional Conference (Turnhalle).
January 1976	International Conference on Namibia and Human Rights is held in Dakar, Senegal.
30 January 1976	UN Security Council unanimously calls on South Africa to take the necessary steps for a transfer of power to the people of Namibia, to allow free elections under UN supervision: Resolution 385 (1976).
18 August 1976	The Constitutional Committee of the Turnhalle reaches agreement on establishing an interim government and an independent Namibia by 31 December, 1978.
20 August 1976	The UN Council for Namibia rejects proposals made by the Turnhalle.
17 September 1976	A three-tier system of government based on "ethnicity" is proposed by Turnhalle.
19 October 1976	Draft resolution in Security Council seeking to impose a mandatory arms embargo on South Africa, denounce the Turnhalle conference and condemn all attempts by South Africa to evade the clear demand of the UN for free elections in Namibia under UN supervision is vetoed by France, UK & US.
1 February 1977	Mr. Martti Ahtisaari is appointed UN Commissioner for Namibia as successor to Mr. S. McBride.
7 April 1977	Approach in Cape Town to the South African Prime Minister by Ambassadors of the Five Western Powers (US, UK, FRG, France, Canada) who are members of the Security Council, to begin negotiations on an internationally acceptable solution to the Namibia question.
27 April 1977	Talks open in Cape Town between the South African Prime Minister and the "Contact Group".
9 May 1977	The Turnhalle Constitutional Committee attends a meeting with representatives of the Contact Group.
16–22 May 1977	International Conference in support of the peoples of Zimbabwe and Namibia held in Maputo, Mozambique.
18 May 1977	South Africa hold referendum of white voters on Turnhalle proposals. 94.69% vote in favour.
19–21 May 1977	South African Prime Minister and US Vice-President confer in Vienna over *inter alia* the question of Namibia.
8–10 June 1977	Second round of talks between South African Prime Minister and Contact Group. South Africa agrees to

suspend plan for an interim government in Namibia and to allow free elections for a constituent assembly, but stalls on the withdrawal of South African troops from the territory.

An Administrator General is to be appointed to administer the territory until elections are held, in cooperation with a UN representative.

1 July 1977	Mr. Nujoma, President of SWAPO, states that SWAPO would accept the appointment of an Administrator General by the UN Council for Namibia provided all South African troops and police are withdrawn and replaced by a UN peacekeeping force.
6 July 1977	Mr. Justice M. T. Steyn is appointed as Administrator General by the South African government.
August 1977	Discussions are held between South Africa and Contact Group in Pretoria, but fail to reach agreement on South African troops withdrawal and the timing of the elections.
8 August 1977	Representatives of the Contact Group and SWAPO confer in New York.
31 August 1977	Proclamation by the South African State President is gazetted in Pretoria reverting the administration of Walvis Bay as from 1.9.77 to Cape Province.
1 September 1977	Justice Steyn takes office as Administrator General in Namibia.
17 October 1977	Further discussions take place between the South African Foreign Minister and Contact Group, and between SWAPO and Contact Group.
7 November 1977	The Turnhalle Constitutional Conference is dissolved in Windhoek.
14 November 1977	The UN Council for Namibia represents SWAPO as newly appointed member of FAO.
Nov–Dec 1977	Meetings between the Contact Group and the South African Foreign Minister and the Contact Group and SWAPO.
Jan–Mar 1978	Western representatives hold "proximity talks", meeting the South African representatives and SWAPO alternatively.
5 April 1978	Western Contact Group submit their plan for a settlement in Namibia to the UN.
25 April 1978	South Africa accepts the plan with reservations over Walvis Bay.

4 May 1978	SA troops attack SWAPO refugee camp at Kassinga in Southern Angola.
June 1978	South Africa embarks on unilateral registration of voters in Namibia.
11–12 July 1978	SWAPO agrees to the Western Plan.
27 July 1978	UN Security Council adopts Resolution 432 (1978) insisting on the reintegration of Walvis Bay with Namibia.
30 August 1978	Dr. Waldheim publishes the Report on the Implementation of the Western Plan.
6 September 1978	The South African Foreign Minister, in a letter to the UN, voices objections to the UN Plan, and insists on elections by 31 December, 1978.
8 September 1978	SWAPO leader Nujoma accepts Waldheim Report "in general" but requests new registration of voters.
20 September 1978	Mr. Vorster resigns as South African Prime Minister. The South African government announces decision to hold elections by the end of the year without UN supervision. P. W. Botha becomes Prime Minister of South Africa.
29 September 1978	The UN Security Council, by Resolution 435, approves the Secretary General's Report.
4–8 December 1978	Internal elections held in Namibia, widely criticised by Namibian churches, SWAPO and other bodies as a fraud. The DTA (a party formed by Turnhalle representatives) wins majority of seats.
16 January 1979	UN Commissioner for Namibia, Mr. M. Ahtisaari, visits Namibia for further consultations on holding second, UN-supervised elections. South Africa demands monitoring of SWAPO bases in Angola and raises other objections.
6 March 1979	Ceasefire beginning proposed by UN for March 15. South African Prime Minister objects to SWAPO bases inside Namibia and denies their existence.
19–23 March 1979	Proximity talks in New York. No progress over South Africa's objections—talks break down.
14 May 1979	The South African Administrator General in Namibia announces transformation of the Namibian Constituent Assembly into a National Assembly with legislative powers, with effect from 21 May, 1979.
13 August 1979	Professor Gerrit Viljoen, chairman of the Broederbond, becomes the new Administrator General in Namibia. UK Ambassador to the UN resumes negotiations with South Africa, putting Angolan proposals of a 50 km wide demili-

tarized zone on either side of the border with Namibia.

November 1979   UN calls proximity talks on Namibia in Geneva to discuss all aspects of the DMZ proposals. SWAPO accepts the concept of a DMZ and declares its readiness to negotiate the technical details, but strongly rejects part of the proposals, including the disarming of or removal to neighbouring countries of its fighters.

December 1979   The South African government accepts the concept of a DMZ, but raises six conditions, including the disarmament of SWAPO personnel.

Nov–Dec 1979   The Administrator General puts forward proposals for strengthening the homelands policy.

February 1980   General Prem. Chand visits Namibia for technical discussions on the DMZ proposals, and has consultations, together with UN Special Representative and other officials, in Cape Town with South African officials, with SWAPO in Angola and with Front Line States governments.

March 1980   Dr. Waldheim publishes report on UN discussions in South Africa and proposes 15 June as target date for implementation.

April 1980   Administrator General visits Britain and is received at the Foreign Office.

12 May 1980   South Africa replies to UN proposals, asking for further assurances relating to 20 South African bases in the DMZ, an increased size of Untag forces in the DMZ and denial of bases to SWAPO.

20 June 1980   Dr. Waldheim informs the South African Minister of Foreign Affairs that, in the best interest of obtaining a final settlement, the Front Line States and SWAPO agree to 20 SA bases, within the framework of the provisions of the Western settlement proposals. He assures SA of the commitment of the Angolan and Zambian governments to ensure that the provisions of the transitional arrangements are respected, and of the complete impartiality of Untag.

Appendix II

LETTER DATED 10 APRIL 1978 FROM THE REPRESENTATIVES OF CANADA, FRANCE, GERMANY, FEDERAL REPUBLIC OF, THE UNITED KINGDOM OF GREAT BRITAIN AND NORTHERN IRELAND AND UNITED STATES OF AMERICA ADDRESSED TO THE PRESIDENT OF THE SECURITY COUNCIL.

On instructions from our Governments we have the honour to transmit to you a proposal for the settlement of the Namibian situation and to request that it be circulated as a document of the Security Council.

The objective of our proposal is the independence of Namibia in accordance with resolution 385 (1976), adopted unanimously by the Security Council on 30 January 1976. We are continuing to work towards the implementation of the proposal.

(signed)

WILLIAM H. BARTON
Permanent Representative of Canada to the United Nations

M. JACQUES LEPRETTE
Permanent Representative of France to the United Nations

RUDIGER VON WECHMAR
Permanent Representative of the Federal Republic of Germany to the United Nations

JAMES MURRAY
Deputy Permanent Representative of the United Kingdom of Great Britain and Northern Ireland to the United Nations, Chargé d'Affairs, a.i.

ANDREW YOUNG
Permanent Representative of the United States of America to the United Nations

Proposal for a settlement of the Namibian situation

I. Introduction

1. Bearing in mind their responsibilities as members of the Security Council of the United Nations, the Governments of Canada, France, the Federal Republic of Germany, the United Kingdom and the United States have consulted with the various parties involved with the Namibian situation with a view to encouraging agreement on the transfer of authority in Namibia to an independent government in accordance with resolution 385 (1976), adopted unanimously by the Security Council on 30 January 1976.

2. To this end, our Governments have drawn up a proposal for the settlement of the Namibian question designed to bring about a transition to independence during 1978 within a framework acceptable to the people of Namibia and thus to the international community. While the proposal addresses itself to all elements of resolution 385 (1976), the key to an internationally acceptable transition to independence is free elections for the whole of Namibia as one political entity with an appropriate United Nations role in accordance with resolution 385 (1976). A resolution will be required in the Security Council requesting the Secretary-General to appoint a United Nations Special Representative whose central task will be to make sure that conditions are established which will allow free and fair elections and an impartial electoral process. The Special Representative will be assisted by a United Nations Transition Assistance Group.

3. The purpose of the electoral process is to elect representatives to a Namibian Constituent Assembly which will draw up and adopt the Constitution for an independent and sovereign Namibia. Authority would then be assumed during 1978 by the Government of Namibia.

4. A more detailed description of the proposal is contained below. Our Governments believe that this proposal provides an effective basis for implementing resolution 385 (1976) while taking adequate account of the interests of all parties involved. In carrying out his responsibilities the Special Representative will work together with the official appointed by South Africa (the Administrator General) to ensure the orderly transition to independence This working arrangement shall in no way constitute recognition of the legality of the South African presence in and administration of Namibia.

II. The electoral process

5. In accordance with Security Council resolution 385 (1976), free elections will be held, for the whole of Namibia as one political entity, to enable the people of Namibia to freely and fairly determine their own future. The elections will be under the supervision and control of the United Nations in that, as a condition to the conduct of the electoral process, the elections themselves, and the certification of their results, the United Nations Special Representative will have to satisfy himself at each stage as to the fairness and appropriateness of all measures affecting the political process at all levels of administration before such measures take effect. Moreover the Special Representative may himself make proposals in regard to any aspect of the political process. He will have at his disposal a substantial civilian section of the United Nations Transition Assistance Group, sufficient to carry out his duties satisfactorily. He will report to the Secretary-General of the United Nations, keeping him informed and making such recommendations as he considers necessary with respect to the discharge of his responsibilities. The Secretary-General, in accordance with the mandate entrusted to him by the Security Council, will keep the Council informed.

6. Elections will be held to select a Constituent Assembly which will adopt a Constitution for an independent Namibia. The Constitution will determine the organization and powers of all levels of government. Every adult Namibian will be eligible, without discrimination or fear of intimidation from any source, to vote, campaign and stand for election to the Constituent Assembly. Voting will be by secret ballot, with provisions made for those who cannot read or write. The date for the beginning of the electoral campaign, the date of elections, the electoral system, the preparation of voters rolls, and other aspects of electoral procedures will be promptly decided upon so as to give all political parties and interested persons, without regard to the political views, a full and fair opportunity to organise and participate in the electoral process. Full freedom of speech, assembly, movement and press shall be guaranteed. The official electoral campaign shall commence only after the United Nations Special Representative has satisfied himself as to the fairness and appropriateness of the electoral procedures. The implementation of the electoral process, including the proper registration of voters and the proper and timely tabulation and publication of voting results will also have to be conducted to the satisfaction of the Special Representative.

7. The following requirements will be fulfilled to the satisfaction of the United Nations Special Representative in order to meet the objective of free and fair elections:

a. Prior to the beginning of the electoral campaign, the Administrator General will repeal all remaining discriminatory or restrictive laws, regulations, or administrative measures which might abridge or inhibit that objective.

b. The Administrator General shall make arrangements for the release, prior to the beginning of the electoral campaign, of all Namibian political prisoners or political detainees held by the South African authorities so that they can participate fully and freely in that process, without risk of arrest, detention, intimidation or imprisonment. Any disputes concerning the release of political prisoners or political detainees shall be resolved to the satisfaction of the Special Representative acting on the independent advice of a jurist of international standing who shall be designated by the Security-General to be legal adviser to the Special Representative.

c. All Namibian refugees or Namibians detained or otherwise outside the territory of Namibia will be permitted to return peacfully and participate fully and freely in the electoral process without risk of arrest, detention, intimidation or imprisonment. Suitable entry points will be designated for these purposes.

d. The Special Representative with the assistance of the United Nations High Commissioner for Refugees and other appropriate international bodies will ensure that Namibians remaining outside of Namibia are given a free and voluntary choice whether to return. Provision will be made to attest to the voluntary nature of decisions made by Namibians who elect not to return to Namibia.

8. A comprehensive cessation of all hostile acts shall be observed by all parties in order to ensure that the electoral process will be free from interference and intimidation. The annex describes provisions for the implementation of the cessation of all hostile acts, military arrangements concerning the United Nations Transition Assistance Group, the withdrawal of South African forces, and arrangements with respect to other organized forces in Namibia, and with respect to the forces of SWAPO. These provisions call for:

a. A cessation of all hostile acts by all parties and the restriction of South African and SWAPO armed forces to base.

b. Thereafter a phased withdrawal from Namibia of all but 1,500 South African troops within 12 weeks and prior to the official start of the political campaign. The remaining South African force would be restricted to Grootfontein or Oshivello or both and would be withdrawn after the certification of the election.

c. The demobilization of the citizen forces, commandos, and ethnic forces, and the dismantling of their command structures.

d. Provision will be made for SWAPO personnel outside of the territory to return peacefully to Namibia through designated entry points to participate freely in the political process.

e. A military section of the United Nations Transition Assistance Group to make sure that the provisions of the agreed solution will be observed by all parties. In establishing the military section of UNTAG, the Secretary-General will keep in mind functional and logistical requirements. The Five Governments, as members of the Security Council, will support the Secretary-General's judgement in his discharge of this responsibility. The Secretary-General will, in the normal manner, include in his consultations all those concerned with the implementation of the agreement. The Special Representative will be required to statisfy himself as to the implementation of all these arrangements and will keep the Secretary-General informed of developments in this regard.

9. Primary responsibility for maintaining law and order in Namibia during the transition period shall rest with the existing police forces. The Administrator General to the satisfaction of the United Nations Special Representative shall ensure the good conduct of the police forces and shall take the necessary action to ensure their suitability for continued employment during the transition period. The Special Representative shall make arrangements when appropriate for United Nations personnel to accompany the police forces in the discharge of their duties. The police forces would be limited to the carrying of small arms in the normal performance of their duties.

10. The United Nations Special Representative will take steps to guarantee against the possibility of intimidation or interference with the electoral process from whatever quarter.

11. Immediately after the certification of election results, the Constituent Assembly will meet to draw up and adopt a Constitution for an independent Namibia. It will conclude its work as soon as possible so as to permit whatever additional steps may be necessary prior to the installation of an independent Government of Namibia during 1978.

12. Neighbouring countries shall be requested to ensure to the best of their abilities that the provisions of the transitional arrangements, and the outcome of the election, are respected. They shall also be requested to afford the neccessary facilities to the United Nations Special Representative and all United Nations personnel to carry out their assigned functions and to facilitate such measures as may be desirable for ensuring tranquility in the border areas.

United Nations Security Council, S/12636, 10 April 1978.

Appendix III

REPORT OF THE SECRETARY-GENERAL SUBMITTED PURSUANT TO PARAGRAPH 2 OF SECURITY COUNCIL RESOLUTION 431 (1978) CONCERNING THE SITUATION IN NAMIBIA

Introduction

1. At its 2082nd meeting on 27 July 1978, the Security Council adopted resolution 431 (1978). By that resolution, the Council, recalling its resolution 385 (1976) and taking note of the proposal for a settlement of the Namibian situation contained in document S/12636 of 10 April 1978, requested me to appoint a Special Representative for Namibia in order to ensure the early independence of Namibia through free elections under the supervision and control of the United Nations. The full text of resolution 431 (1978) reads as follows:

> *The Security Council,*
>
> *Recalling* its resolution 385 (1976) of 30 January 1976, taking note of the proposal for a settlement of the Namibian situation contained in document S/12636 of 10 April 1978,
>
> 1. *Requests* the Secretary-General to appoint a Special Representative for Namibia in order to ensure the early independence of Namibia through free elections under the supervision and control of the United Nations.
>
> 2. *Further requests* the Secretary-General to submit at the earliest possible date a report containing his recommendations for the implementation of the proposal in accordance with Security Council resolution 385 (1976);
>
> 3. *Urges* all concerned to exert their best efforts towards the achievement of independence by Namibia at the earliest possible date.

2. Immediately following the decision of the Security Council, I appointed Mr. Martti Ahtisaari, the United Nations Commissioner for Namibia, as my Special Representative for the purposes of the resolution.

3. Mindful of the Council's further request contained in paragraph 2, I requested my Special Representative to undertake, at the earliest possible date, a survey mission to Namibia for the purpose of gathering for me all the information necessary for the preparation of the present report. To assist him in this task. I placed at his disposal a team of United Nations officials and military advisers.

4. This report, which is based on the survey of my Special Representative, is submitted to the Security Council in accordance with paragraph 2 of resolution 431 (1978), in which the Council requested the Secretary-General "to submit at the earliest possible date a report containing recommendations for the implementation of the proposal in accordance with Security Council resolution 385 (1976)".

I. The survey mission

5. As stated above, my Special Representative, accompanied by a staff of United Nations officials and military advisers, visited Namibia from 6 to 22 August for the purpose of carrying out a survey of all matters relative to the implementation of resolution 431 (1978).

6. In addition to meetings with the Administrator-General of the Territory and his staff, as well as with the South African military and police commanders and local authorities, the Special Representative had the opportunity to consult extensively with representatives of political parties, churches, the business community and individuals. His consultations in this regard covered a wide spectrum of public opinion within the Territory. In this connexion, the Special Representative and his staff, by travelling extensively within the Territory, were able to familiarize themselves with local conditions which would have relevance to the effective organisation and operation of a United Nations Transition Assistance Group entrusted with the tasks set out in the proposal for a settlement of the Namibian situation contained in document S/12636.

7. In the course of his meetings and consultations, the Special Representative was able to obtain the view of not only the Administrator-General and his staff but the representatives of the Namibian people on a broad range of important topics relating to the necessary conditions for the holding of free and fair elections and to the role of the United Nations. Among the principal subjects discussed were the repeal of all the remaining discriminatory or restrictive laws, regulations or administrative measures which might abridge or inhibit the objective of free and fair elections; arrangements for ensuring the release of political prisoners and detainees, as well as the voluntary return of Namibians; the arrangements and dispositions required to ensure the cessation of all hostile acts; the electoral process; the composition and work of the Constituent Assembly; and the time-table for the accomplishment of the above stages. The military aspects of the operation, with special reference to the introduction and functioning of the military component of the United Nations Transition Assistance Group, were also fully discussed. In addition, the Special Representative also discussed with the Administrator-General the manner of ensuring the good conduct of the police and the arrangements necessary to assure the free and unrestricted discharge by the United Nations staff of the tasks assigned to them.

II. General guidelines

8. The implementation of the proposal in paragraph 2 of resolution 431 (1978) will require the establishment of a United Nations Transition Assistance Group (UNTAG) in the Territory, consisting of a civilian component and a military component. Because of the unique character of the operation and the need for close co-operation between them, both components will be under the over-all direction of the Special Representative of the Secretary-General.

9. The Special Representative will report to me, keeping me informed and making such recommendations as he considers necessary with respect to the discharge of his responsibilities. The Secretary-General, in accordance with the mandate entrusted to him by the Security Council, will keep the Council fully informed of developments relating to the implementation of the proposal and to the functioning of UNTAG. All matters which might affect the nature or the continued effective functioning of UNTAG will be referred to the Council for its decision.

10. The deployment of both components of UNTAG must take into account the specific geographic, demographic, economic and social conditions prevailing in Namibia. These include, in particular, the vast distances and varied nature of topography and vegetation; the broad ranges of climatic conditions; the scarcity of water; the population distribution and existing communication network; the distribution and concentration of ethnic groups; and the lack of an adequate infrastructure in the north, such as roads and other communications and facilities. All these factors, when analysed, make it evident that sizeable resources, both military and civilian, will be required to provide the close monitoring called for in document S/12636.

11. In performing its functions, UNTAG will act with complete impartiality. In order that the proposal may be effectively implemented, it is expected that the Administrator-General and all other officials from within the Territory will exhibit the same impartiality.

12. For UNTAG to carry out all its tasks effectively, three essential conditions must be met. First, it must, at all times, have the full support and backing of the Security Council. Second, it must operate with the full co-operation of all the parties concerned, particularly with regard to the comprehensive cessation of all hostile acts. Third, it must be able to operate as a combined United Nations operation, of which the military component will constitute an integrated, efficient formation within the wider framework of UNTAG.

13. To monitor the cessation of hostilities effectively, to maintain surveillance of the Territory's vast borders and to monitor the restriction to base of the armed forces of the parties concerned, the co-operation and support of the neighbouring countries will be necessary. Such co-operation will be most important, particularly during the early stages.

14. Implementation of the proposal, and thus the work of UNTAG, will have to proceed in successive stages. These stages, which are detailed in the annex to document S/12636, can be grouped as follows:

a. Cessation of all hostile acts by all parties and the withdrawal, restriction or demobilization of the various armed forces;

b. Conduct of free and fair elections to the Constituent Assembly, for which the pre-conditions include the repeal of discriminatory or restrictive laws, regulations or administrative measures, the release of political prisoners and detainees and voluntary return of exiles, the establishment of effective monitoring by the United Nations and an adequate period for electoral campaigning;

c. The formulation and adoption of a constitution for Namibia by the Constituent Assembly;

d. The entry into force of the constitution and the consequent achievement of independence of Namibia.

15. The length of time required for these stages is directly related to the complexity of the tasks to be performed and to the overriding consideration that certain steps are necessary before it can be said that elections have been held under free and fair conditions. It will be recalled that the proposal envisaged a series of successive stages, spaced so as to provide a sufficient lapse of time before the holding of the elections. This should permit, among other things, the release of political prisoners and detainees, the return and registration of all Namibians outside the Territory who may wish to participate in the electoral process, the deployment of United Nations military and civilian personnel and electoral campaigning by all parties in an atmosphere of tranquility. The time-table set out in the proposal called for the lapse of approximately seven months from the date of the approval of the present report by the Security Council to the holding of the elections.

16. In his discussions with the Special Representative, the Administrator-General said that the South African authorities, having previously established 31 December 1978 as the date of independence, felt that they were committed thereto and that, consequently, the elections should take place as scheduled, regardless of the fact that it would necessitate substantially reducing the time-table necessary for completion of the preparatory plans. A majority of the political parties was of the opinion, however, that it was essential to maintain the orderly phasing of the preparatory stages and to allow sufficient time for electoral campaigning in order to ensure free and fair elections. Further, it was pointed out that the actual date of independence would fall within the competence of the Constituent Assembly.

17. It will be recalled, however, that at the time the proposal was first formulated, the date of 31 December 1978 was consistent with completion of these steps. The delay in reaching agreement among the parties now makes completion by this date impossible. It is therefore recommended that the transitional period begin on the date of approval of the present report by the Security Council and proceed in accordance with the steps outlined in document S/12636. Using the same time-table that earlier provided the 31 December 1978 date, an appropriate date for elections would be approximately seven months from the date of the approval of the present report.

18. Estimates of the periods of time required for completion of stages (a) and (b) of paragraph 14 above are included in the annex to document S/12636. In view of the fact that the periods required for stages (c) and (d) of paragraph 14

would be determined by the Constituent Assembly, it is expected that the duration of UNTAG would be one year, depending on the date of independence to be decided by the Constituent Assembly.

19. UNTAG will have to enjoy the freedom of movement and communication and other facilities that are necessary for the performance of its tasks. For this purpose UNTAG and its personnel must necessarily have all the relevant privileges and immunities provided by the Convention on the Privileges and Immunities of the United Nations, as well as those especially required for the proposed operation.

20. The military component of UNTAG will not use force except in self-defence. Self-defence will include resistance to attempts to prevent it from discharging its duties under the mandate of the Security Council. UNTAG will proceed on the assumption that all the parties concerned will co-operate with it and take all the necessary steps for compliance with the decisions of the Security Council.

III. Establishment of UNTAG

A. Military component

21. The functions which will be performed by the military component of UNTAG are set out in paragraph 8 of document S/12636 and in the annex thereto. These include, in particular:

a. Monitoring the cessation of hostile acts by all parties, the restriction of South African and SWAPO armed forces to base, the phased withdrawal of all except the specified number of South African forces and the restriction of the remainder to specified locations;

b. Prevention of infiltration as well as surveillance of the borders of the Territory;

c. Monitoring the demobilization of citizen forces, commandos and ethnic forces, and the dismantling of their command structure.

22. The military component will assist and support the civilian component of UNTAG in the discharge of its tasks.

23. The military component of UNTAG will be under the command of the United Nations, vested in the Secretary-General, under the Authority of the Security Council. The command in the field will be exercised by a Commander appointed by the Secretary-General with the consent of the Security Council. The Commander will report through the Special Representative to the Secretary-General on all matters concerning the functioning of the military component of UNTAG.

24. The military component will be comprised of a number of contingents to be provided by member countries upon the request of the Secretary-General. The contingents will be selected in consultation with the Security Council and with the parties concerned, bearing in mind the accepted

principle of equitable geographical representation. In addition, a body of selected officers to act as monitors will form an integral part of the military component.

25. The military component, including the monitors, will be provided with weapons of a defensive character consistent with the guidelines set out in paragraph 20 above.

26. In order that the military component might fulfil its responsibilities, it is considered that it should have a strength of the order of seven infantry battalions, totalling approximately 5,000, plus 200 monitors and in addition, command, communications, engineer, logistic and air support elements totalling approximately 2,300. The infantry battalions should be fully self-sufficient.

27. It will be essential to establish an adequate logistic and command system at the very outset of the operation. It will therefore be necessary to obtain urgently from Governments the elements of such a system. In this connexion, it may well be necessary to use also the services of civilian contractors for some logistic functions, as appropriate. In the nature of the physical circumstances pertaining to this operation, UNTAG may have to rely to a considerable extent on existing military facilities and installations in Namibia.

B. Civilian component

28. The civilian component will consist of two elements. One of these elements will be the civil police, whose function will be to assist the Special Representative in implementing the tasks set out in paragraphs 9 and 10 of document S/12636.

29. The duties of the civil police element of UNTAG will include taking measures against any intimidation or interference with the electoral process from whatever quarter, accompanying the existing police forces, when appropriate, in the discharge of their duties and assisting in the realization of the function to be discharged by the Administrator-General to the satisfaction of the Special Representative of ensuring the good conduct of the existing police forces.

30. In order that the UNTAG police may fulfil their responsibilities, as described above, it is considered, as a preliminary estimate, that approximately 360 experienced police officers will be required. It is hoped that police officers will be made available by Governments on a secondment basis, bearing in mind the accepted principle of equitable geographical representation, as well as the language and other requirements of the assignment.

31. The non-police element of the civilian component of UNTAG will have the function of assisting the Special Representative in implementing paragraphs 5 to 7 of document S/12636 and the relevant sections of the annex thereto. These tasks will consist, in particular, of the following:

84

a. Supervising and controlling all aspects of the electoral process, considering the fairness and appropriateness of the electoral procedures, monitoring the balloting and the counting of votes, in order to ensure that all procedures are strictly complied with, and receiving and investigating complaints of fraud or challenges relating to the electoral process:

b. Advising the Special Representatives as to the repeal of discriminatory or restrictive laws, regulations of administrative measures which may abridge or inhibit the objective of free and fair elections;

c. Ensuring the absence of, or investigating complaints of, intimidation, coercion or restrictions on freedom of speech, movement or peaceful political assembly which may impede the objective of free and fair elections;

d. Assisting in the arrangements for the release of all Namibian political prisoners or detainees and for the peaceful, voluntary return of Namibian refugees or Namibians detained or otherwise outside the Territory;

e. Assisting in any arrangements which may be proposed by the Special Representative to the Administrator-General and implemented by the Administrator-General to the Special Representative's satisfaction intended to inform and instruct the electorate as to the significance of the election and the procedures for voting.

32. Bearing in mind the vast size of the Territory, the dispersal of the population and the lack of adequate communications, it is considered, as a preliminary estimate, that approximately 300 Professional officers, as well as the necessary supporting staff, will be required initially until the cessation of hostile acts has been achieved. Thereafter about 1,000 Professional and 200 field service and General Service staff will be required during the electoral campaign and the period of balloting in order to cover all the polling stations. The staff will, among other duties, be required for 24 regional centres and more than 400 polling stations.

33. It is anticipated that some of these officials will be provided from among existing United Nations staff and that some will be persons appointed especially for this operation. In addition, it is my hope that a significant number of officials can be seconded or loaned by Governments. All such seconded or loaned personnel will be required to assume the responsibilities incumbent on United Nations officials.

34. It is also my intention to conduct consultations concerning the designation of a jurist of international standing whose appointment as legal adviser to the Special Representative is provided for in paragraph 7B of document S/12636.

IV. Proposed plan of action

35. Subject to the approval of the present report by the Security Council, it is my intention to initiate the operation as quickly as possible.

36. It is my intention to appoint as Commander of the military component of UNTAG Major-General Hannes Philipp, who has extensive experience of

United Nations peace-keeping operations and is already familiar with the situation in Namibia.

37. Immediately following such a decision by the Security Council, the Special Representative, accompanied by the Commander of the military component, the key elements of their staffs together with essential command and logistic elements, will proceed to Namibia in order to establish the headquarters of UNTAG and begin operations as quickly as possible.

38. A number of Governments have already expressed their interest in providing military contingents for UNTAG. Immediately upon the approval of the present report by the Security Council, it is my intention to consult the Council and the parties concerned on the composition of the military component, bearing in mind the principle of equitable geographical representation, on the one hand, and the necessity of obtaining self-sufficient units, on the other. Every effort will be made to begin the deployment of the military component within 3 weeks and to bring it to its full strength within 12 weeks. For this to be achieved, it will be necessary to determine the composition of the military component at the earliest possible time.

39. It is also my intention to approach Governments to provide military personnel to serve as monitors. In the initial stages, given the urgency of deploying at least some of the monitors, it may be possible to draw upon officers already serving with other existing United Nations operations. This may also apply to key staff positions.

40. As regards civilian personnel, it is likewise my intention, as stated in paragraphs 30 and 33 above, to approach Governments to make available on secondment or loan experienced police officers to serve as police monitors and other experienced officials to serve in the civilian component of UNTAG. In recruiting civilian staff for UNTAG, I shall bear in mind both the accepted principle of equitable geographical representation and the urgent need to deploy a large number of experienced staff within the shortest possible time.

V. Financial implications

41. At present there are too many unknown factors to permit an accurate assessment of the cost of UNTAG. Based on the numbers of personnel specified in this report and the envisaged duration of 12 months, and taking into account the magnitudes and elements of the financial requirements experienced in other peace-keeping operations, the indications are that the financial requirements for UNTAG could be as high as $300 million. Of this, approximately $33 million will be required to finance the return of refugees and exiles. In view of the nature of the operation, due regard should be given to the fact that some elements of the operation might be phased out before the end of the mandate and that alternative arrangements might be possible which could result in lower costs.

42. The costs of UNTAG shall be considered expenses of the Organization to be borne by the Member States in accordance with Article 17, paragraph 2, of the Charter.

United Nations Security Council S/12827, 29 August 1978.

Appendix IV

Statement—Herman ja Toivo

Statement by Herman ja Toivo, a founder member of SWAPO and accused No. 24, after he was found guilty of offences under the Terrorism Act by the Supreme Court in Pretoria on 26 January, 1968. He and 36 other Namibians were charged with having participated in a conspiracy to overthrow the existing Government of Namibia, receiving guerilla training and practising guerilla warfare.

My Lord,

We find ourselves here in a foreign country, convicted under laws made by people whom we have always considered as foreigners. We find ourselves tried by a judge who is not our countryman and who has not shared our background.

When this case started, counsel tried to show that this court had no jurisdiction to try us. What they had to say was of a technical and legal nature. The reasons may mean little to some of us, but it is the deep feeling of all of us that we should not be tried here in Pretoria.

You, my Lord, decided that you had the right to try us, because your parliament gave you that right. That ruling has not and could not have changed our feelings. We are Namibians and not South Africans. We do not now, and will not in the future recognise your right to govern us; to make laws for us in which we had no say; to treat our country as if it were your property and as if you were our masters. We have always regarded South Africa as an intruder in our country. This is how we have always felt and this is how we feel now, and it is on this basis that we have faced this trial.

I speak of "we" because I am trying to speak not only for myself, but for others as well, and especially for those of my fellow accused who have not had the benefit of any education. I think also that when I say "we", the overwhelming majority of non-white people in South West Africa would like to be included.

We are far away from our homes; not a single member of our families has come to visit us, never mind be present at our trial. The Pretoria gaol, the Police Headquarters at Compol, where we were interrogated and where statements were extracted from us, and this court is all we have seen in Pretoria. We have been cut off from our people and the world. We all wondered whether the headmen would have repeated some of their lies if our people had been present in court to hear them.

The South African government has again shown its strength by detaining us for as long as it pleased; keeping some of us in solitary confinement for 300 to 400 days and bringing us to the capital to try us. It has shown its strength by passing an Act especially for us and having it made retrospective. It has even chosen an ugly name to call us by. One's own are called patriots, or at least rebels; your opponents are called terrorists.

A court can only do justice in political cases if it understands the position of those that it has in front of it. The State has not only wanted to convict us, but also to justify the policy of the South African government. We will not even try to present the other side of the picture, because we know that a court that has not suffered in the same way that we have, cannot understand us. This is perhaps why it is said that one should be tried by one's equals. We have felt from the very time of our arrest that we were not being tried by our equals but by our masters, and that those who have brought us to trial very often do not even do us the courtesy of calling us by our surnames. Had we been tried by our equals, it would not have been necessary to have any discussion about our grievances. They would have been known to those set to judge us.

It suits the government of South Africa to say that it is ruling South West Africa with the consent of its people. This is not true. Our organisation, SWAPO, is the largest political organisation in South West Africa. We considered ourselves a political party. We know that whites do not think of blacks as politicians—only as agitators. Many of our people, through no fault of their own, have had no education at all. This does not mean that they do not know what they want. A man does not have to be formally educated to know that he wants to live with his family where he wants to live, and not where an official chooses to tell him to live; to move about freely and not require a pass; to earn a decent wage; to be free to work for the person of his choice for as long as he wants; and finally to be ruled by the people that he wants to be ruled by, and not by those who rule him because they have more guns than he has.

Our grievances are called "so-called" grievances. We do not believe South Africa is in South West Africa in order to provide facilities and work for non-whites. It is there for its own selfish reasons. For the first forty years it did practically nothing to fulfil its "sacred trust". It only concerned itself with the welfare of the whites.

Since 1962, because of the pressure from inside by the non-whites and especially my organisation, and because of the limelight placed on our country by the world, South Africa has been trying to do a bit more. It rushed the Bantustan Report so that it would at least have something to say at the World Court.

Only one who is not white and has suffered the way we have can say whether our grievances are real or "so-called".

Those of us who have some education, together with our uneducated brethren, have always struggled to get freedom. The idea of our freedom is not liked by South Africa. It has tried to prove through the mouths of a couple of its paid chiefs and a paid official that SWAPO does not represent the people of South

West Africa. If the government of South Africa were sure that SWAPO did not represent the feelings of the people of South West Africa, it would not have taken the trouble to make it impossible for SWAPO to advocate its peaceful policy.

South African officials want to believe that SWAPO is an irresponsible organisation that resorts to the level of letting people not get vaccinated. As much as White South Africans may want to believe this, this is not SWAPO. We sometimes feel that it is what the Government would like SWAPO to be. It may be true that some members or even members of SWAPO somewhere refused to do this. The reason for such refusal is that some people in our part of the world have lost confidence in the governors of our country and they are not prepared to accept even the good that they are trying to do.

Your Government, my Lord, undertook a very special responsibility, when it was awarded the mandate over us after the First World War. It assumed a sacred trust to guide us towards independence and to prepare us to take our place among the nations of the world. We believe that South Africa has abused that trust because of its belief in racial supremacy (that White people have been chosen by God to rule the world) and apartheid. We believe that for fifty years South Africa has failed to promote the development of our people. Where are our trained men? The wealth of our country has been used to train your people for leadership and the sacred duty of preparing the indigenous people to take their place among the nations of the world has been ignored.

I know of no case in the last twenty years of a parent who did not want his child to go to school if the facilities were available, but even if, as it was said, a small percentage of parents wanted their children to look after cattle, I am sure that South Africa was strong enough to impose its will on this, as it has done in many other respects. To us it has always seemed that our rulers wanted to keep us backward for their benefit.

1963 for us was to be the year of our freedom. From 1960 it looked as if South Africa could not oppose the world for ever. The world is important to us. In the same way as all laughed in court when they heard that an old man tried to bring down a helicopter with a bow and arrow, we laughed when South Africa said that it would oppose the world. We knew that the world was divided, but as time went on it at least agreed that South Africa had no right to rule us.

I do not claim that it is easy for men of different races to live at peace with one another. I myself had no experience of this in my youth, and at first it surprised me that men of different races could live together in peace. But now I know it to be true and to be something for which we must strive. The South African government creates hostility by separating people and emphasising their differences. We believe that by living together, people will learn to lose their fear of each other. We also believe that this fear which some of the whites have of Africans is based on their desire to be superior and privileged and that when whites see themselves as part of South West Africa, sharing with us all its hopes and troubles, then that fear will disappear. Separation is said to be a natural process. But why then is it imposed by force, and why then is it that whites have the superiority?

Headmen are used to oppress us. This is not the first time that foreigners have tried to rule indirectly—we know that only those who are prepared to do what their masters tell them become headmen. Most of those who had some feeling for their people and who wanted independence have been intimidated into accepting the policy from above. Their guns and sticks are used to make people say they support them.

I have come to know that our people cannot expect progress as a gift from anyone, be it the United Nations or South Africa. Progress is something we shall have to struggle and work for. And I believe that the only way which we shall be able and fit to secure that progress is to learn from our own experience and mistakes.

Your Lordship emphasised in your judgement the fact that our arms come from communist countries, and also that words commonly used by communists were to be found in our documents. But my Lord, in the documents produced by the State there is another type of language. It appears even more often than the former. Many documents finish up with an appeal to the Almighty to guide us in our struggle for freedom. It is the wish of the South African government that we should be discredited in the Western world. That is why it calls our struggle a communist plot; but this will not be believed by the world. The world knows that we are not interested in ideologies. We feel that the world as a whole has a special responsibility towards us. This is because the land of our fathers was handed over to South Africa by a world body. It is a divided world, but it is a matter of hope for us that it at least agrees about one thing—that we are entitled to freedom and justice.

Other mandated territories have received their freedom. The judgement of the World Court was a bitter disappointment to us. We felt betrayed and we believed that South Africa would never fulfil its trust. Some felt that we would secure our freedom only by fighting for it. We knew that the power of South Africa is overwhelming, but we also knew that our case is a just one and our situation intolerable—why should we not also receive our freedom?

We are sure that the world's efforts to help us in our plight will continue, whatever South Africans may call us.

We do not expect that independence will end our troubles, but we do believe that our people are entitled—as are all peoples—to rule themselves. It is not really a question of whether South Africa treats us well or badly, but that South West Africa is our country and we wish to be our own masters.

There are some who will say that they are sympathetic with our aims, but that they condemn violence. I would answer that I am not by nature a man of violence and I believe that violence is a sin against God and my fellow men. SWAPO itself was a non-violent organisation, but the South African government is not truly interested in whether opposition is violent or non-violent. It does not wish to hear any opposition to apartheid. Since 1963, SWAPO meetings have been banned. It is true that it is the tribal authorities who have done so, but they work with the South African government, which has never lifted a finger in favour of political freedom. We have found ourselves voteless in our own country and deprived of the right to meet and state our own political opinions.

Is it surprising that in such times my countrymen have taken up arms? Violence is truly fearsome but who would not defend his property and himself against a robber? And we believe that South Africa has robbed us of our country.

I have spent my life working in SWAPO which is an ordinary political party like any other. Suddenly we in SWAPO found that a war situation had arisen and that our colleagues and South Africa were facing each other on the field of battle. Although I had not been responsible for organising my people militarily and although I believe we were unwise to fight the might of South Africa while we were so weak, I could not refuse to help them when the time came.

My Lord, you found it necessary to brand me as a coward. During the Second World War, when it became evident that both my country and your country were threatened by the dark clouds of Nazism, I risked my life to defend both of them, wearing a uniform with orange bands on it.

But some of your countrymen when called to battle to defend civilisation resorted to sabotage against their own fatherland. I volunteered to face German bullets, and as a guard of military installations, both in South West Africa and the Republic, was prepared to be the victim of their sabotage. Today they are our masters and are considered the heroes, and I am called the coward.

When I consider my country, I am proud that my countrymen have taken up arms for their people and I believe that anyone who calls himself a man would not despise them.

In 1964 the ANC and PAC in South Africa were suppressed. This convinced me that we were too weak to face South Africa's force by waging battle. When some of my country's soldiers came back I foresaw the trouble there would be for SWAPO, my people and me personally. I tried to do what I could to prevent my people from going into the bush. In my attempts I became unpopular with some of my people, but this, too, I was prepared to endure. Decisions of this kind are not easy to make. My loyalty is to my country. My organisation could not work properly—it could not even hold meetings. I had no answer to the question "Where has your non-violence got us?" Whilst the World Court judgement was pending, I at least had that to fall back on. When we failed, after years of waiting, I had no answer to give to my people.

Even though I did not agree that people should go into the bush, I could not refuse to help them when I knew that they were hungry. I even passed on the request for dynamite. It was not an easy decision. Another man might have been able to say "I will have nothing to do with that sort of thing." I was not, and I could not remain a spectator in the struggle of my people for their freedom.

I am a loyal Namibian and l could not betray my people to their enemies. I admit that I decided to assist those who had taken up arms. I know that the struggle will be long and bitter. I also know that my people will wage that struggle, whatever the cost.

Only when we are granted our independence will the struggle stop. Only when our human dignity is restored to us, as equals of the whites, will there be peace between us.

We believe that South Africa has a choice—either to live at peace with us or to subdue us by force. If you choose to crush us and impose your will on us then you not only betray your trust, but you will live in security for only so long as your power is greater than ours. No South African will live at peace in South West Africa, for each will know that his security is based on force and that without force he will face rejection by the people of South West Africa.

My co-accused and I have suffered. We are not looking forward to our imprisonment. We do not, however, feel that our efforts and sacrifice have been wasted. We believe that human suffering has its effect even on those who impose it. We hope that what has happened will persuade the whites of South Africa that we and the world may be right and they may be wrong. Only when white South Africans realise this and act on it, will it be possible for us to stop our struggle for freedom and justice in the land of our birth.

References

The following abbreviations are used:

BBC   British Broadcasting Corporation Monitoring Service.
CT   Cape Times, Cape Town.
Debates   South African House of Assembly Debates (Hansard).
FOCUS   FOCUS on Political Repression in Southern Africa, IDAF news bulletin.
FM   Financial Mail, Johannesburg.
FT   Financial Times, London.
GN   Guardian, London.
MS   Morning Star, London.
Obs   Observer, London.
RDM   Rand Daily Mail, Johannesburg.
SALB   South African Labour Bulletin, Durban.
Star   Star Weekly Airmail edition, Johannesburg.
ST   Sunday Times, Johannesburg.
T   The Times, London.
Tel   Daily Telegraph, London.
WA   Windhoek Advertiser, Windhoek.
WO   Windhoek Observer, Windhoek.

I. FACTS AND FIGURES

1. *WA* 29.10.70.
2. *Southern Africa* May 1979, p. 8.
3. *Towards Manpower Development for Namibia—Background Notes*, United Nations Institute for Namibia, 1978, p. 1.
4. W. H. Thomas *Economic Development in Namibia—Towards Acceptable Development Strategies for Independent Namibia*, Kaiser Grunewald 1978, p. 19.
5. South African Department of Foreign Affairs, *South West Africa* Survey 1974. According to SA estimates, the population of Namibia increased by 2.7% since 1970 to an estimated 946,000. *Johannesburg radio broadcast, BBC* 18.7.80.
6. W. H. Thomas, *Economic Development in Namibia* op. cit. p. 20. Of the 11 non-white "population groups" designated by South Africa, the Nama, Rehoboth Basters and Coloureds are classified as "Coloured" for administrative purposes, while the others are termed "African" or "Bantu". In this text, unless South African classifications are used to explain South African policies, the term "black" refers to all non-white Namibians.

II. HISTORY

1. W. Nachtwei, *Namibia*, Sendler 1976, p. 19–22.
2. *Ibid.*, pp. 35, 48.
3. *Ibid.*, pp. 39, 60.
4. *Ibid.*, p. 31.
5. J. H. Wellington, *South West Africa and its Human Issues*, Oxford 1967, p. 231.
6. W. Nachtwei, op. cit., p. 39.
7.. J. H. Wellington, op. cit., p. 196.
8. M. O'Callaghan, *Namibia, the effects of apartheid on culture and education*, UNESCO, Paris 1977 p. 18.
9. H. Bley, *German South West Africa*, in: Segal and First (ed.), *South West Africa, Travesty of Trust*, London 1967.
10. M. O'Callaghan, op. cit., p. 19.
11. J. H. P. Serfontein, *Namibia*, London, 1976, p. 21.
12. South African Administration's Report to the Permanent Mandate's Commission, 1928.

III. THE INTERNATIONAL STATUS OF NAMIBIA

1. Information on SWAPO. *SWAPO: An Historical Profile*, published by SWAPO Department of Information and Publicity, Lusaka (Zambia) 1978, p. 15.
2. *Bulletin of the African Institute of South Africa*, No. 6/7, Pretoria 1977, p. 185.
3. *Africa*, No. 8, 1978, p. 20.
4. GN 7.8.78.
5. *Ibid.*
6. The Council, originally composed of 11 members, was enlarged to 18 members in 1972, to 25 members in 1974 and to 31 members in 1978. Today the Council is composed of the following countries: Algeria, Angola, Australia, Bangladesh, Belgium, Botswana, Bulgaria, Burundi, Chile, China, Columbia, Cyprus, Egypt, Finland, Guyana, Haiti, India, Indonesia, Liberia, Mexico, Nigeria, Pakistan, Poland, Romania, Senegal, Turkey, Union of Soviet Socialist Republics, United Republic of Cameroon, Venezuela, Yugoslavia and Zambia.
In accordance with standing arrangements, the representative of the South West Africa People's Organisation (SWAPO), which has permanent observer status in the United Nations General Assembly, participates in the work of the Council for Namibia. The Organisation of African Unity (OAU) also participates in the work of the Council for Namibia in an observer capacity.
7. *Report of the United Nations Council for Namibia* (A/7338), New York 1968.
8. UN Institute for Namibia, 1980.
9. *Ibid.*, p. 21–22.
10. *Namibia Bulletin*, United Nations, 1/77.

IV. SOUTH AFRICAN POWERS AND POLICIES

1. L. Lazar, *Namibia*, published by The Mandate Trust, Africa Bureau, London 1972, p. 17.

2. International Labour Office, *Labour and Discrimination in Namibia,* Geneva 1977, p. 22.
3. *Ibid.,* p. 23.
4. *Ibid.,* p. 24.
5. M. O'Callaghan, *Namibia, the effects of apartheid on culture and education,* op. cit., p. 50.
6. *Ibid.,* p. 51.
7. *WA* 9.2.77.
8. *WA* 1.5.77.
9. *WA* 7.2.77.

V. APARTHEID IN PRACTICE

1. J. H. P. Serfontein, *Namibia,* op. cit., p. 39.
2. *WA* 6.2.79.
3. ILO, *Labour and Discrimination in Namibia,* op. cit., p. 47. According to statistics given in the SA media, the number of teachers in black schools more than doubled between 1970 and 1979 to reach 4,596. The number of black children receiving secondary education had increased from 2,000 to 12,000 during the same period, according to that source. *Johannesburg radio* 16.7.80, reported by BBC 18.7.80.
4. *WA* 6.2.79.
5. *Action in Namibia,* Bulletin of the Namibia Support Committee, London, Nov/Dec 1979.
6. *CT* 24.7.79.
7. Debates, 25.5.77.
8. Population Census May 1970, Republic of South Africa Dept. of Statistics.
9. W. Nachtwei, *Namibia,* op. cit., p. 106.
10. *South West Africa Survey 1974,* op. cit.
11. W. Nachtwei, *Namibia,* op. cit., p. 106.
12. W. H. Thomas, *Economic Development in Namibia,* op. cit., p. 23.
13. United Nations Council for Namibia, *Social Conditions in Namibia,* (A/AC. 131/L.52), August 1977, p. 16.
14. G. and S. Cronje, *The Workers of Namibia,* International Defence and Aid Fund, London Feb 1979, p. 62
15. *WA* 21.9.79.
16. *WO* 29.3.80.
17. SALB Vol. 4 Nos 1 and 2, Jan–Feb 1978.
18. *The view from the shop floor,* in: SALB, ibid.
19. *Constitutional Conference of South West Africa,* Cape Town 1976, p. 29.
20. Africa Bureau *Fact Sheet No. 23,* Oct 1972.
21. *WA* 18.2.75.
22. L. Lazar, *Namibia,* op. cit., p. 28.
23. W. Nachtwei, *Namibia,* op. cit., p. 77.
24. UN Commission on Human Rights, *Situation of Human Rights in Southern Africa,* Report of the Ad Hoc Group of Experts (E/CN.4/1222) 31.1.1977, p. 109.
25. UN Commission on Human Rights, *Violation of Human Rights in Southern Africa,* Progress Report of the Ad Hoc Working Group of Experts (E/CN.4/1270) 31.1.1978, p. 105.

VI. THE ECONOMY

1. *Report of the UN Council for Namibia No. 24* (A/10024)., Vol. I, 1976, p. 26.

2. Africa Bureau *Fact Sheet No. 51* May/June 1979.
3. *Report of the UN Council for Namibia,* Vol. I, 1976, op. cit., p. 32.
4. *Ibid.* p. 25.
5. Cronje & Cronje, *The Workers of Namibia,* op. cit., p. 15.
6. *ST* 9.9.79.
7. African Business, Sept 1979.
8. United Nations Department of Political Affairs, Trusteeship and Decolonization: *Decolonization* No. 9/revised edition. December 1977, Issue on Namibia, p. 13.
9. *WA* 30.11.79.
10. R. Green, *Towards Manpower Development for Namibia, Background Notes* p. 39.
11. W. Schneider-Barthold, *Namibia's economic potential and existing economic ties with the Republic of South Africa,* German Development Institute, Berlin 1977, p. 22.
12. *FM* 31.8.79.
13. Report of the United Nations Council for Namibia, Vol. I, 1976, op. cit., p. 32.
14. *Ibid.*
15. *WA* 3.5.78.

VII. THE LABOUR FORCE

1. R. H. Green, *Towards Manpower Development for Namibia—Background Notes,* op. cit., p. 6.
2. *Ibid.,* Table 6.
3. *Ibid.,* Table 4.
4. Cronje and Cronje, op. cit., p. 22.
5. *Ibid.,* p. 26.
6. *Ibid.,* p. 39.
7. W. H. Thomas, *Economic Development in Namibia,* op. cit., p. 197, Table 22.
8. *WA* 1.2.78.
9. *Star* 4.2.78.
10. *RDM* 22.3.78.
11. *WA* 20.3.80.
12. *BBC* 9.4.80.
13. R. Green, op. cit., p. 19.
14. Report of the United Nations Council for Namibia, Vol. I, 1976, op. cit., p. 34.
15. R. Green, op. cit., p. 19.
16. *SALB,* op. cit., p. 98.
17. *WA* 14.6.78.
18. *SALB,* op. cit., p. 97.
19. *ILO* op. cit., p. 61.
20. Cronje and Cronje, op. cit., p. 47.
21. *FM* 1.9.78.
22. Cronje and Cronje, op. cit., p. 77.
23. *Ibid.,* p. 92.
24. *RDM* 29.12.78.
25. *Namibia Today,* No. 2, 1979, p. 16.
26. *FT* 21.4.79.
27. *WA* 3.9.79.

VIII. THE DENIAL OF HUMAN RIGHTS

1. *FOCUS* No. 14, January 1978, p. 2; No. 22, May–June 1979, p. 15; No. 23, July–August 1979, p. 2.
2. *FOCUS* No. 25, Nov–Dec 1979, p. 16.
3. UN Commission on Human Rights (E/CN.4/1222) op. cit., p. 111.
4. *WA* 1.5.79.
5. *FOCUS* No. 24, Sept–Oct 1979, p. 14.

6. *WO* 30.6.79.
7. *SWAPO Information on Namibian Political Prisoners,* SWAPO Department of Information and Publicity, Lusaka (Zambia), 1978, p. 4.
8. *Namibia Today,* No. 3, 1979.
9. *FOCUS* No. 21, March–April 1979, p. 7.
10. *SWAPO News Brief,* London 25.7.79.
11. *WA* 28.1.80.
12. *WO* 15.3.80.
13. *SWAPO Information on Namibian Political Prisoners,* op. cit., p. 26.
14. Africa Bureau *Fact Sheet* No. 35, April 1974.
15. *FOCUS* No. 9, March 1977, p. 15.
16. *FOCUS* No. 10, May 1977, p. 18.
17. *WA* 16.11.78.
18. *WA* 3.8.78.
19. *WA* 7.8.78.
20. *WA* 27.7.78.
21. *GN* 28.5.77.
22. United Nations Working Group of Experts (E/CN.4/1270) op. cit., p. 110.
23. *Ibid.*
24. *Ibid.,* p.111. For detailed evidence of torture in Namibia, see *Torture, a Cancer in our Society,* publ., by Catholic Institute of International Relations and British Council of Churches, 1978.
25. *FOCUS* No. 24, Sept–Oct 1979, p. 14.
26. Speech by *Lucia Hamutenya* to Satis (South Africa—the imprisoned society) Conference, London, 9.2.80.
27. *Testimony to the Ad Hoc Working Group of Experts on Human Rights in London,* 16 July 1974, given by SWAPO.
28. *SWAPO Information on Namibian Political Prisoners,* op. cit., p. 10.
29. *Ibid.,* p. 10.
30. UN Commission on Human Rights, *The Situation of Human Rights in Southern Africa,* Report of the Ad Hoc Working Group of Experts (E/CN.4/1050), 2 February 1971, para. 243.
31. UN Working Group of Experts, (E/CN.4/1222) op. cit., p. 113.
32. *SWAPO Information on Namibian Political Prisoners,* op. cit., p. 16.
33. *Ibid.,* p. 114.
34. *Ibid.*
35. *SWAPO News Brief,* London 25.7.79.
36. *Debates,* 10.3.80.
37. *SWAPO Information on Namibian Political Prisoners,* op. cit., p. 11.
38. *WA* 23.5.80.
39. *SWAPO Information on Namibian Political Prisoners,* op. cit., p. 11–15.
40. *WO* 2.2.80, *WA* 30.1.80, *WA* 15.2.80, *BBC* 12.3.80.

IX. CONTROL OF THE PRESS AND THE MEDIA

1. *RDM* 13.11.78.
2. *Ibid.*
3. *WA* 23.11.78.
4. *RDM* 29.11.78.
5. *RDM* 5.5.79.
6. *WO* 6.10.79.
7. *WA* 27.11.79
8. *BBC* 1.5.79.

9. *WA* 11.10.79.
10. *WA* 15.6.79

X. THE CHURCH

1. M. O'Callaghan, *Namibia, the effects of apartheid on culture and education,* op. cit., p. 95.
2. Programme to Combat Racism (PCR) Information, *Namibia—Recent Developments,* No. 2, 1979, p. 8, in: Lutheran World Federation, *Information,* 18.12.79.
3. S. Groth, *A Question of Conscience,* in: *Event,* Vol. 14, No. 2, Feb/March 1974, p. 7.
4. J. H. P. Serfontein, *Namibia?* op. cit., p. 210.
5. *Open Letter to the Administrator General, Justice M. T. Steyn,* 3.5.79, from the Council of Churches in Namibia.
6. *FOCUS* no. 24, Sept–Oct 1979, p. 14.
7. *GN* 15.7.78.
8. *FOCUS* No. 24, Sept–Oct 1979, p. 14.
9. J. H. P. Serfontein, *Namibia?* op. cit., p. 212–213.

XI. POLITICAL GROUPINGS

1. SWAPO Information on SWAPO: *A Historical Profile,* publ. by SWAPO Department of Information and Publicity, Lusaka (Zambia), July 1978.
2. *FOCUS* No. 27, March–April 1980, p. 4.
3. Africa Bureau *Fact Sheet* No. 48, July/August 1978.
4. *Africa,* September 1978.
5. *Namibia, a Unique Responsibility.* Highlights of UN action in support of Freedom and Independence for Namibia. UN Department of Public Information (DPI/631), undated, p. 15.
6. Africa Bureau *Fact Sheet* No. 48, op. cit.
7. *Constitution of the South West Africa People's Organisation,* adopted by the meeting of the Central Committee, July 28—August 1, 1976, Lusaka, Zambia. *Article III, Aims and Objectives.*
8. *WO* 12.4.80.
9. *WA* 23.2.79.
10. *Star,* 10.2.79.
11. *RDM* 7.12.79.
12. *WA* 24.3.80.
13. *Star* 23.9.79.
14. In reply to a question in parliament, the South African Prime Minister listed the departments transferred to the control of the Administrator General by end of January, 1980:
Agricultural Credit and Land Tenure
Agricultural Economics and Marketing
Agricultural Technical Services
Co-operation and Development
Education and Training
Coloured, Rehoboth and Nama Relations
Commerce and Consumer Affairs
Community Development
Finance
Forestry
Health
Industries
Information Service of South Africa
Inland Revenue
Interior
Justice
Manpower Utilization

Mines
National Education
Posts and Telecommunications
Prisons
Public Works
Social Welfare and Pensions
Statistics
Sport and Recreation
Transport Affairs
Water Affairs
(South Africa Government Gazette, 7.2.80, p.
12).
15. *WO* 8.9.79.
16. *RDM* 25.7.79.
17. *WA* 26.7.79.
18. *S. Express,* 12.8.79.
19. *WA* 18.4.80.
20. *WA* 21.9.79.
21. *WA* 22.6.79.
22. M. Vesper, *Uber die Beziehungen zwischen
BRD und Namibia,* ISSA No. 19, February
1980.
23. *WA* 9.10.78.
24. *RDM* 11.5.78.
25. *WO* 7.7.79.
26. *WO* 24.2.79.
27. *S. Express,* 12.8.79.

XII. THE WAR IN NAMIBIA

1. *Namibia Review,* publ., by Namibia Study
Group, Student African Movement, Johannesburg, 1978, p. 35.
2. *Ibid.,* p. 38.
3. *Namibia Today,* publ., by SWAPO Department of Information and Publicity, Lusaka
(Zambia), No. 3, 1979, p. 16.
4. *Debates* 11.5.79.
5. *Press Conference with Per Sanden,* London,
10.5.78.
6. M. Garoeb, SWAPO Administrative Secretary, *Speech to Conference of the International
Committee against Apartheid, Racism and
Colonialism in Southern Africa (ICSA),*
Stockholm, 11.4.80.
7. *WA* 11.2.80.
8. *T* 22.4.80.
9. *FOCUS* No. 23, July-August 1979, p. 1.
10. Cronje and Cronje, *The Workers of Namibia,*
op. cit., p. 84.
11. *Namibia Bulletin,*1/77, p. 8.
12. *Action on Namibia,* op. cit., May–June 1979.
13. *Star* 21.7.79.
14. *FOCUS* No. 20, Jan–Feb 1979, p. 16.
15. *GN* 19.5.79.
16. *Agence France Presse,* 1.6.79.
17. *Namibia Bulletin* 2/79, p. 21.
18. M. Garoeb, op. cit.
19. *WO* 15.12.79.
20. *WA* 27.3.80.
21. *Namibia Update,* 15.7.79, publ. by United
States National Committee of the Lutheran
World Federation, New York.
22. *FOCUS* No. 23, July-August 1979, p. 1.
23. *WA* 15.6.79.
24. *WA* 7.9.79.
25. *WA* 3.6.80.
26. *RDM* 18.10.79.
27. *ST* 19.8.79.

28. *WO* 8.9.79.
29. *GN* 25.6.79.
30. *Namibia Today,* 2/78, *GN* 6.5.78.
31. United Nations Security Council (S/13473)
*Report on the Human Casualties and Material
and other damage resulting from repeated acts of
aggression by the racist regime of South Africa
against the People's Republic of Angola,*
25.7.79.
32. *BBC* 20.9.79.
33. *UN Weekly Summary,* London 3.7.80.
34. *WO* 8.3.80.
35. J. H. P. Serfontein, *Namibia?* op. cit., p. 229.
36. *Children into Exile,* International Defence and
Aid Fund, London 1979.
37. *Ibid.*

XIII. ALTERNATIVE STRATEGIES

1. See *All Options or None,* IDAF Fact Paper No.
3, August 1976.
2. United Nations Security Council Resolution
385, 30.1.76.
3. In September 1976, the UN Security Council
met to review South Africa's compliance with
the demands made in Resolution 385. A formal
call by Third World states for a mandatory
arms embargo against South Africa was vetoed
by the US, Britain and France on the grounds
that substantial progress was being made
towards reaching a peaceful solution. (*SAIRR,
A Survey of race relations in South Africa,
1976,* p. 478). During December 1976, the
Security Council was again urged to consider
the imposition of an arms embargo. The
resolution was opposed by six countries
including the US, France, Britain and West
Germany, (*Ibid*).
4. SAIRR, op. cit., 1977, pp. 595–604.
5. UN Security Council Resolution 431, 27.7.78.
6. UN Security Council Resolution 435, 29.9.78.
7. J. Ellis, *Elections in Namibia,* British Council
of Churches and Catholic Institute for International Relations, May 1979.
8. *FT* 7.9.78.
9. UN Security Council Resolution 439 of
13.11.78. UN General Assembly Resolution
33/182B of 21.12.78.
10. *Report on the Registration and Election
Campaign in Namibia, 1978,* by the Christian
Centre, Namibia, 28 November 1978.
11. J. Ellis, op. cit.
12. *WA* 4.7.79.
13. *BBC* 28.6.80, *WA* 24.6.80.
14. *WA* 4.7.79.
15. *Citizen* 3.6.80, *WA* 1.7.80, Proclamation
AG19, Establishment and Powers of a Council
of Ministers for South Africa, 12.6.80.
16. *WA* 20.6.80, *WA* 24.6.80.
17. *WA* 13.12.79.
18. Statement by Sam Nujoma, President of
SWAPO, in Geneva, 16.11.79.
19. *WO* 3.4.80, see also *Free Elections in
Namibia—Postponed indefinitely,* A briefing
on the failure of Western diplomacy, Action on
Namibia occasional paper No. 3 in cooperation
with IDAF, May 1980.
20. *WO* 17.5.80.
21. *WA* 24.6.80.
22. *T* 24.6.80.

Selected Bibliography and suggestions for further reading

Facts and Figures

A detailed geographical survey of Namibia is contained in J. H. Wellington, *SWA and its human issues* (Clarendon Press, Oxford 1967), though the book's political leanings are clearly pro-South African. For a critical analysis of population statistics see W. H. Thomas, *Economic Development in Namibia* (Kaiser-Grunewald 1978), and P. Fraenkel, *The Namibians of SWA*, a Minority Rights Group Report No. 19. (1974). See also R. H. Green, *Manpower estimates and development implications for Namibia*, published by the UN Institute for Namibia (Lusaka, Zambia 1978).

Namibian History

Chapters on pre-colonial history are contained in JHP Serfontein, *Namibia?* (Fokus Suid Publishers 1976) and Wellington, see above. A German book by W. Nachtwei *Namibia* (Sendler1976) deals with Namibia's pre-colonial society and of African resistance against German and S.A. rule.

German occupation and SA rule under the League of Nations Mandate are dealt with in these publications, and in Fraenkel's booklet (see above).

R. Vigne, *A Dwelling Place of our Own*, (International Defence and Aid Fund 1975), deals with important events in Namibia's history.

South African rule in Namibia

The Africa Bureau have produced a *Fact Sheet No. 23* on the Bantustan policy. M. O'Callaghan, *Namibia, the effects of apartheid on culture and education*, (UNESCO 1977) deals with the history of racial discrimination in these fields.

The UN Council for Namibia has published a *Report on Social Conditions in Namibia* (A/AC. 131/L.52, 26.8.1977), dealing with education, health and housing conditions in Namibia.

Racial legislation, the suppression of human rights and labour restrictions are dealt with in G. & S. Cronje, *The Workers of Namibia*, published by the International Defence and Aid Fund (1979), *Labour and discrimination in Namibia*, published by the International Labour Organisation (Geneva 1977), and SWAPO, *Information on Namibian Political Prisoners* (1978).

The Economy

W. H. Thomas, *Economic Development in Namibia*, (Kaiser Grünewald 1978), W. Schneider-Bertholt, *Namibia's Economic Potential and Existing Economic Ties with the Republic of South Africa* (German Development Institute 1977), *The Mineral Industry of Namibia*, R. Murray (Commonwealth Secretariat London 1979).

The Churches

Marion O'Callaghan's book, *Namibia, the effects of apartheid on Culture and Education* (UNESCO 1977) deals briefly with the early missionary presence in Namibia and extensively with the churches' involvement in education. J. H. P. Serfontein *Namibia?* has a chapter on the churches' political involvement and protest against the violation of human rights. See also Colin Winter's autobiography, *Namibia—the story of a bishop in exile,* (Lutterworth Press, London, 1977).

Political Groupings

For a brief history of SWAPO, see *SWAPO, An Historical Profile* (SWAPO Information 1978). For other political parties, see J. H. P. Serfontein, *Namibia?*

Settlement Negotiations

All Options and None, a Fact Paper published by the IDAF (August 76) analyses the progress of the Turnhalle talks. Justin Ellis, *Elections in Namibia,* (British Council of Churches and Catholic Institute for International Relations May 1979), covers the 1978 elections. *Namibia—negotiations and "elections",* published by SIDA Area Division (Stockholm 1979) and L. Lazar, *Namibia* (Africa Bureau 1972) cover Namibia's international status.

The War in Namibia

SWAPO: An Historical Profile (SWAPO Information, 1978) and *On the Peoples' Resistance* 1976-1977 (SWAPO Information, 1978) chronicles the development of the liberation struggle. *The Apartheid War Machine,* IDAF *Fact Paper No. 8* 1980, has information on South Africa's military involvement in Namibia and Angola.

Current Developments

The South African Institute of Race Relations publishes an annual *Survey of Race Relations in South Africa* which includes a section on Namibia, giving a wealth of factual detail of the year's events.

Up to date information on the situation in Namibia, such as military developments, repressive legislation, arrests etc., can be found in the bi-monthly bulletin *FOCUS* published by the IDAF, and the *Namibia Bulletin,* published quarterly by the United Nations Council for Namibia. This also contains information on UN activities on Namibia. The UN Council for Namibia publishes periodic reports on specific aspects of the country. Publications of support groups include *Action on Namibia,* a monthly journal by the Namibia Support Committee, London, and *Anti-Apartheid News,* the monthly newspaper of the British Anti-Apartheid Movement. SWAPO publishes *Namibia Today* and *Information and comments,* a collection of press articles and comments by SWAPO-UK office.

Index